I0116571

SITTING ON A RACIAL VOLCANO

(Guyana Uncensored)

G.H.K. LALL

Copyright © 2013 G.H.K Lall
All rights reserved.

ISBN: 0615787444
ISBN-13: 9780615787442

Also By GHK Lall

Guyana: A National Cesspool of Greed, Duplicity & Corruption
(A Remigrant's Story)

Writing as Hilary Kincaid

Soaring into Magnificence —From Illness to Holiness
Birth of the Millennium —A Walk through Life's Pathways

DEDICATIONS

To all patriotic Guyanese who long for something different
To Melissa Sarah and Samara Sara
And to Ruth
Yes, all things are indeed possible.

TABLE OF CONTENTS

AUTHOR'S NOTES

Several decisions had to be made for this writing. The first was easy: no racial slurs in the descriptions. Thus, the major races are identified as "Indian" and "Black." In terms of the latter group, it was felt that 'Negro' would be both misplaced and somewhat anachronistic; and "African" or "Afro-Guyanese" both suffer from lack of widespread usage, and are still somewhat awkward locally. Also, Black is capitalized throughout. But no pejoratives in any instance; this would do more harm than good.

The second decision was not to relive the disturbances and atrocities of the 60s through regurgitation; it is believed that this would be a distraction, as well as counterproductive. There is the occasional passing allusion to those times, but no more. Instead, the focus is on the recent past and today; and what this period has generated-or not generated-in respect of inclusion and harmony, and its significance for the future.

Third, the local Creolese is kept to a minimum. Standard English is the standard employed. Fourth, the term "race" is used throughout, as opposed to "ethnic." Race is the word Guyanese know and use; it is how they converse or describe anything related. Additionally, apologies are in order for taking the easy way out and settling for expressions that are androcentric, hence gender biased.

Sixth, this effort focuses on the two major races, which comprise that 75–80% of the population coexisting uneasily, if not carefully, resentfully, and angrily. Arguably, hatefully, too.

Also, reference is made continuously to the "PNC" as representative of the opposition, Black people, and Guyanese. This might be problematic for some, given recent developments leading up to the 2011 elections. I persist.

Next, this work is the product of hundreds of conversations with family, friends, neighbors, colleagues, acquaintances, strangers, and declared (some) foes from all walks of life; thousands of interactions with Guyanese here and those resident overseas; and a lifetime of observation of who and how and what many really are beneath the surface and at the core. It is the stark etchings of dreams abandoned, dignity demolished, and fears harbored. ALL AS EXPRESSED. Because the circumstances occur in a small space, and players operate on multiple platforms, and at many levels, there is some overlap and unavoidable repetition.

Finally, it is hoped that others will be encouraged, and inspired to be even more candid on this touchiest of subjects. It is time that this story is told.

PREFACE

"Shall we say all is well? Shall we continue to praise by force of habit or practice that which is wrong? We would ruin the country ..."
-Robespierre

Guyana and Guyanese are always a short distance away from a fateful racial brink. It is a place that first ensnares and then catapults, one and all, past the last feeble restraints to beyond the point of return. This is the grim specter of a future that threatens, endangers, and unhinges. No one is listening ...

This is neither prophecy nor vision. Rather, it is a concerned citizen daring to discern and issuing a very public warning, many warnings. It is a thankless occupation. I am interpreting as I see the circumstances of the present and what they project for the future, while being well aware of the great difficulties that litter the way ahead. These range from the potentially sanguinary to the nationally convulsive. I wish that I could envision a different future: one that is about building instead of plundering; gathering together rather than dividing; inculcating the richness of dreams, as opposed to the bleakness of hopelessness; and working towards uplifting all-repeat all-instead of merely some.

I must confess to a deepening cynicism, a creeping sense of despair, even though at heart I am an optimist, and a believer in the irrepressible spirit of man. There is no unique sophistication involved in what I present; only a dogged willingness to shed light on suppressed truths.

In view of my own passage in this life-where I come from, where I have been and where I find myself today-I can channel all of this into a probably highly disputatious, undesired scrutiny of the national soul. If this is the clashing color of my own outlook, then it must be asked: what about the less fortunate? How do they react to their circumstances? What are their expectations? What will be their destiny?

As the hard, sharp questions and realities of race, politics, and destiny are tabled, the urgent need for inclusive embrace will not be recognized, and any such recommendation not be welcome. This is so, even though it is well-known that at several crucial, very tense junctures in the history of this nation, full scale deterioration was averted by a hairsbreadth. Threadbare terms and agreements rescued the moment and the nation from collapse into the abyss of the unknown. Society survived to drag itself on hands and knees into another dismal day; an endless succession of dismal days for the many. This was lauded in some quarters as victory, as progress.

Since then, there have been continuing sentiments verbalized of sellout to the enemy, and failure to deliver the *coup de grace* to a nemesis reeling on the ropes. Thus, there has been only surly acceptance-if acceptance is indeed the word-of political compromises reached, at the grassroots level. It is a shaky, paltry peace that is prone to rupture when subject to a minimum of stress. This is made worse by claims of lack of implementation, along with unending reciprocal accusations of chronic bad faith and overarching guile.

These conditions are representative of hard words, harder feelings, and still harder realities. Undeniable realities. And this is best captured and summed up in this manner: The peoples of Guyana sit on top of a known, restless, threatening volcano. It is called RACE. There is no way to sugarcoat, ignore, or dismiss this prowling, mindless monster in the midst. Anyone who looks the other way, or pretends otherwise may rightly be considered reckless, if not lacking in good sense. This nation has endured its share of the occasional racial eruption, the rush of consuming lava, the sweep of threatening peril; but these have been explosions in miniature, and only a precursor of greater dangers currently harnessed, and still ahead. Still, the burns and scars and memories are painful to the flesh, and irremovably embedded.

Let there be no quibbling, hedging or grudging partial understanding. Race lies at the hub and heart of this society. Its spokes and arteries are easily recognized in the practice of politics, the existence of division, and the specter of fear. All of this is presented in this writing in stark, jolting terms. In fact, another title for this book could have been: "*Bitter Racial Realities in Guyana –A Primer for Tragedy.*" It is believed appropriate.

A few will point to surging, climactic tension during national elections in an effort to link and limit the strength and depth of feelings to a recurring quadrennial event, and only then and that. They are out of touch with reality. Matters simply move from a furious boil on the front-burner to a slow simmer on the backburner in the post-election interval. Others will hustle for the convenient-but specious-comfort offered through utterances of "extremists." This is the height of vapidity, grossly inaccurate, even a deliberate falsehood, as the piercing discontent and rage is neither miniscule in number nor negligible in content. And while political rulers see it fit to race past the muted day-to-day animosities with the gloss and pontification of imaginary brotherhood and unity, this only enrages further, and solves nothing. It is a calculated distortion, a red herring by first the black man, and now the brown ones.

Unsurprisingly, the kinetic energy levels-the racial heat-in the local volcano intensifies. It stirs and flexes contained, but growing, strength. There have been warning spasms and belches, but no outright eruption in boiling splashing fury. All that happens is that below the surface poisons thicken and heave. Impatiently. Disturbingly. Dangerously. Sooner or later (and it might not be much later) the pent-up forces of frustration and rage will shatter restraints and blow away those in the path. It could likely be smartly marshaled and well-distributed, which would be destructive enough. A larger holocaust looms if it is unannounced, uncontrolled, and unknown in origin. Then there is no awareness, or grasp, or measurement as to where any roads lead. None whatsoever, at any level, and in all corners. These are the undercurrents present in today's Guyana. They point to a bleak, disturbing future.

The sensitive are forewarned of the apocalypse that looms in this beloved country's future. There is heaviness and resignation; there was once the forlorn hope that the national destiny would be different; the ingredients to make this a reality are, however, largely lacking. Instead, there is so much smugness, arrogance, resistance, deviousness, and the usual terrible miscalculation. This is true of the two major parties that have, regrettably, a place and stake in the today and tomorrow of this society. Of necessity, and as powered by domestic realities, this writing takes both the PPP and PNC to task; in their hands reside the keys to Guyana's kingdom, except that each has misused egregiously the trust and responsibility. Neither is spared.

As said earlier, what is written is what has been seen, heard, discerned, and lived. Call it the twin geniuses of being there and a modicum of common sense, amidst the scorching latitudes of the equator. It is the terrifying fateful abyss to which this nation has marched, over which it leans in growing restlessness and danger. There is the belief that volcanic eruption and cataclysm is inevitable: As sure as the sun rises in the East, such a cataclysm promises a harsh brutal reckoning that will lay bare this pretended, tortured racial existence.

Like every decent, thinking, patriotic Guyanese, the fervent wish is that things would be different. But how can this be when close to two out of five of local residents-all of one race-are relegated and condemned to the humiliating existence of depending, of waiting, and, of sometimes, begging? How can it be when even the well-nourished members of the dominant race fortify themselves through foreign exit strategies? How can it be otherwise when the out-of-power group knows of the flashpoints and chokepoints that can bring this society to its knees, disrupt the false calm that has existed for so long, and shatter the harness of the oppressor that binds? And, make no mistake, it is how this is seen, perceived, discussed, and accepted: as hated oppression, despised oppressors, and a crippling, but removable, yoke. There is the possibility of limited inaccuracy, but it is what is perceived. And perception is strength, perception is fact, perception is trouble.

We can wish all we want that the patriotic (whoever and wherever they are), the powerful, and the pragmatic will be less tribal and more inclusive, more embracing and less divisive. Such a wish might be realized for a short time, then what? In the eye of the mind, there is seen only tumult and peril. There have been fleeting skirmishes, bullets dodged, and worrying times. But that is all there were: skirmishes and temporary respites. I believe that this society is firmly, irreversibly set for a long delayed rendezvous with destiny. All indications are that such a destiny will be abundant in anguish, devastating in impact, and catastrophic in final result. It is part of the continuing retardation of leadership, suspension of sanity, absence of fairness, and suppression of the rational and conscience.

A word of clarification is in order at this point: This is neither sociology study nor political science exercise nor expert undertaking. Even if it were, there is the substantial risk that too many-as in some polls-would present answers that are bland, noncommittal, or misleading. Stated differently, responses would be that which makes for easy listening and ready acceptance, but are far from the truth. There should be nothing groundbreaking here, except the discomfort and controversy generated by exposing some of the unwashed racial undergarments in full public view. The language is muted, but the delicate are cautioned.

GHK Lall -April 2013

PART I

The Position: A Sharp, Angry Existence

PROLOGUE

"Tame the savageness of man and make gentle the life of this world."
-Aeschylus

Yesterday – The way we were

Absorb this scene from several years ago, as it unfolded on a street in Georgetown. Two children are locked in a juvenile battle; they are on the cusp of teenage years at a maximum. They wrestle and pummel each other, while a sparse crowd gathers. An adult male comes to an abrupt halt on his bicycle and peers over the head of the thin crowd and uttered these memorable, meaningful words: "Is two straight hair, leh deh kill deh self." He just as quickly went his way. No one should be at a loss as to the racial heritage of the two "straight hair" lads, or the dismissive, callous adult. But just in case: the former were Indians, and the latter a Black Guyanese. One must wonder as to his reaction if it was a mixed-race (Black-Indian) fight.

Not too long after, and this time in a village, there is this tableau. It is the immediate aftermath of a motor vehicle accident. Bystanders are busy settling back to a state of normalcy, but the evidence of the collision is still lying around on the roadway. A small open-back truck slows down; it is well populated with standing Indian males. They dispassionately survey the wreckage strewn on the shoulder of the road, then shout out "How much black maan ded?" Then they were gone in a roar of acceleration, and a cloud of exhaust smoke.

Here are two telling incidents from yesteryear; two out of likely many not dissimilar ones. What does each tell? Can these be accurately, realistically viewed as isolated? Or aberrations? Or misplaced ignorance and hostility? Maybe, maybe not. Can it be said that citizens-and none more so than the major, competing races-are more enlightened, more tolerant, more embracing these days? Can they be, given that since the time of these two incidents there is the sullied history, the crippling cargoes of rigging and pretended cross-racial support; of divisive elections (and surrounding racial tensions and violence); of heinous crimes and massacres; of protecting and protected phantoms squads; of white collar roguery; of political strangulation and vulgarities; and of drug empires among endless farragoes of wrongdoing and injustice? How have matters changed for the better when race and piercing racial concerns are present in almost every aspect of Guyanese life? Or on what basis stands any fleecy claims of exaggeration, when two leaders had this to say recently?

In January, 2013, the Honorable Speaker of the House used a sharp, terrifying phrase to emphasize the dangers in pursuing a particular course related to amendments before the National Assembly. The phrase he used was "civil war" that could come the next day, if the government's amendments were allowed to be tabled. Less than two months later, the president himself seized the expediency of place and moment at Babu John to speak in ringing tones of "hate" and "haters." The words employed by both leaders represent singularly amazing and inspired examples of unprecedented political frankness; both will be examined at length in due course. Remember these expressions: "civil war" alongside "hate" and "haters." What could be said clearly right now is that this society is perched on the edge of a volcanic storm. And just as clearly, no matter how dismissed and by whom, something extraordinarily powerful and sinister lies beneath the surface calm. It is something far reaching in sweep and destructive in potential for all citizens. And it centers on race; it is nourished by race; it is propelled by race.

In this introductory recitation, that which has plagued and horrified has generated certain irreversible beliefs: That there is a damning, irrefutable racial component in Guyanese life; that it haunts, terrifies, and enrages; that is grows quietly, but determinedly; and that it promises a terrible calamity for the peoples of this society. The bottom line is that there is a racial volcano that burns deep within; it is one that is recklessly stoked; and through its very presence and muted heat generates a spirit of continual agitation. Now it is time for a harder, closer look; a brutal look. As Guyanese read and absorb, they should ask a few simple, but tough, questions: For the most part, is this not who and how we really are? Is this not how we have always been and have allowed ourselves to be? Is there any likelihood of us being substantially different in the future? And is there truly any hope for us to survive intact as one nation?

CHAPTER I

Today ~ The Way We Are

"Oh! Had I the ability .... I would today put out a fiery stream of biting ridicule .... We need the storm, the whirlwind, the earthquake."
-Frederick Douglass

What has changed from yesterday, if anything? Has anything new and refreshing developed on the racial front? Has there been growth in understanding and acceptance as individuals, groups, and a nation? Is there due recognition of mutual indispensability rather than more of the old mutual intolerance and insanity? The answers must be a resounding "NO!" over and over again. From all appearances, matters are worse than before, lines are more rigidly and sharply drawn, and beliefs more deeply embedded. The racial tinderbox is never cool to the touch. There is now an invisible sign that warns the unwary or bold: Stay Away. Keep a Safe Distance. Know your place. Stay with your own kind. It is the way of today. At another level, the politically correct era has fostered public hypocrisy, and multiplied private hostility. Citizens venture forth carefully in a land heavily overcast with muted hostility and reciprocal dislike.

On the Edge of a Perilous Slope

"I am ashamed." "I am angry." "I am sickened." "I am fearful."

These are some of the verbatim expressions heard or shared with astonishingly regularity. They are from real people, and span the spectrum of race, occupations, and social station. Shame and anger and disgust have been shared by doctors, attorneys, students, housewives, shop assistants, taxi drivers, laborers, and many others. The youthful and the mature, the poor and the successful, the educated and the not well-read, as well as members of the racial rainbow have all been bold enough-and honest enough-to articulate their deep misgivings and an abiding anxiety. Most of the anger and disgust is expressed by Black Guyanese; and the fear by both Blacks and Indians, but mainly Indians.

These are thinking, concerned patriots who are solid, successful citizens on the one hand, and the multitude of struggling and despairing at the bottom of the ladder on the other. It is a long bottom. They are not fringe elements or cranks; they are not extremists.

What do all of these powerful feelings mean? To where do they lead? Can this society discover itself, discover sanity and reason, and stave off threatened disaster? Is anyone listening? If they are, do they care?

Two Mindsets: Minority and Multitude

For starters, two things must be said here and now. Both are unpalatable, both will make many squirm in discomfort, advance a believed mitigating defense. First, the contented, well-positioned people are those who stake out and carve out an existence from the ugliness of the times. These include, for the most part, the unspeakably corrupt, the rich-and growing richer-profiteers of a system and environment gone terribly awry. This tiny minority could be venal politicians and cronies, and those individuals who seek their association and blessings; shady businesspeople; and shadowy movers of narcotics, arms, money, or people. Sometimes, it is the same people who are engaged in these prosperous activities. In short, those who make a killing financially-sometimes literally-from the way things are. The well-settled, well-lubricated, well-protected, and sometimes well-respected like this way of life, and all that it offers and has made possible. THEY DO NOT WANT CHANGE. The status quo is beautiful, constructive, and rewarding. Lavishly so. Why change! To hell with change!

This well established minority is powerfully entrenched and slightly diversified racially; it is predominantly Indian. The position of this new pigmentocracy is clear and simple: This is the life. It is the first ugly truth of local life, and a source of sharp resentments and building trouble.

The second unpalatable-even dismissed-truth is that race impacts, resonates and transcends the body, mind, and soul of Guyanese existence. Deliberately or casually, philosophically or emotionally, race permeates Guyanese days, ways, thinking, actions, and outlook. In too many communities and for too many individuals this is the alpha and omega. Race serves as rationale and stimulus for division, agony, anxiety, and fear. Race is the high octane ingredient that powers hate; it knows neither reason, nor unity, nor vision of a shared future. It is the jaundiced color of the past and the overpowering stench of the present. It is rarely invisible, though it is sometimes intangible. Even in the best of times (the skimpiest of moments), race hovers on the near and distant periphery-like faint thunder-in the consciousness of the overwhelming majority of citizens. It threatens; it infuses dread.

All of this spells trouble for this country and its inhabitants. In many ways, these two unmentionable, and searing truths, embody the immovable object of the prosperous and comfortable versus the irresistible force of the have-nots, the sidelined, the denied, and the ignored. And throughout, there is RACE functioning as foundation, vision, and accelerant. Race will be the tide of inevitable convergence-indeed, confrontation and conflict-in the future of Guyana. It is a future that holds an impenetrable grimness where the satisfied few are pitted against the enraged despairing many in a clash of destinies; the former are Indian, the latter Black. And trapped in the middle of this developing convulsion are the innocents, the forgotten, the dismissed, the manipulated, the vulnerable, and the resigned who are Black and Indian and Amerindian. It goes without saying that given the complexion and content of conflict none would be spared.

Here in this heaving milieu-the promise of the future-are thinking Indians who were once, still are, firm supporters of the racial flag. They meander in various states of disillusionment; they are demoralized and distressed; they are concerned and apprehensive. But the flag will not be abandoned; separation yes, divorce no. Remember: these are thinking, conscientious Indians.

Here are the resentful and increasingly furious Black Guyanese. They simmer in silence, in protest, in mounting frustration. They feel marginalized and betrayed; they see themselves relegated to bottom-feeders and outsiders. Their place, development, and aspirations are dependent on the whims and moods of others; their dignity is subject to the goodwill of the determinedly paternalistic. None of this is anywhere near good enough; most of it is far from satisfactory or acceptable; all of it burns the psyche and soul with increasing heat.

Despair gives way to distrust. In time, distrust intensifies into fear. And invariably, the latter leads to extreme prejudice, even hate. This is easily, reflexively reciprocated in a multiplicity of forms and channels. The origins can be traced to a dispiriting history. The inheritance is the tarnished barren present. The solution lies in the looming, promised ruptures of a grim future. In the interim, individual discontent, racial misgivings, and community tensions grow and build inexorably. They grow and build unacknowledged and unaddressed ....

Three Huge Running Sores in the Psyche – The First Three Only

Where will circumstances lead? How long can that which exists hold? What does it mean for this society and its peoples? It is opportune to make a quick, early foray into three revealing areas (three only) that together tell the whole story: elections, crime, and corruption. Each has bred massive insecurities and towering wrath, which conditions the reactions of both segments, and conditions the thinking and views of one for the other.

The cellophane-thin mask is never more abruptly shed than during national elections, when the raw, true nature of the competing power blocs-read races- are exposed to the illumination of observation. Whether instigated or natural, even the blind and somewhat comatose can sense the naked racial tensions, the sudden racial distance, no matter how well camouflaged, if anyone cared to do so. It just is there like a smoldering, collapsible wall thickly coated with the fear of violence and mayhem.

Some of this is stoked, some intrinsic, some learned. It is unnerving and disturbing.

Sure, the ugliness reluctantly subsides in the long aftermath of these bitter contests. But here is the key: the ugliness and bitterness never disappears substantially in the face of loss and loss of identity; in the surge of anticipation and the despair of disappointment: the boiling racial pot slides from the heat of the moment to the humid wasteland of suspension, where it bubbles and sputters unattended. In effect, it is a temporary, tactical retreat characterized more by exhaustion and uncertainty, than by any rethinking and reinvention. In sum, nothing is learned, nothing is gained, and nothing is changed. During these tempestuous times, only the sturdiest and most authentic of cross-racial relationships avoid, and navigate successfully, the surging pounding waves of victory and defeat. The rest of the peoples of this nation go their ways. And those ways are distinctly separate.

But this is during elections. What about day-to-day? How are Indian and Black Guyanese in some of the challenges and developments of daily life?

In homes and communities and strongholds, there can be no denying a sense of secret satisfaction when a blow against the other group is struck, through successful, hugely rewarding criminal incidents; when the depredations of a "Blackie" or "Fineman" wreak havoc; when the rampages of a Khan and phantoms are unleashed to counter, neutralize, and overcome enemies. How many can obscure a visceral delight when fearsome stalkers are eliminated, many times in very questionable circumstances? None should doubt that race is not a feature-and a significant one-in this "get them" and "get-back-at-them" mentality, in the hidden calculus. *They might be terrorists to the other side, but they are our terrorists.*

Then, there are the frustrations of daily interactions heaped high by congestion, competition, traffic aggressiveness, and deliberate disdain. Both sides saunter, walk, jaywalk, ride, drive, park as they please to the detriment and inconvenience of all, but with particular disregard for members of the other race. It is obvious, it is provocative, and it skates on narrow margins and thinning tempers. The invitation is clear: "knack me and yuh gun see wha gun happen ..." And "screw you too! Screw all ah ya'all." There is stare-down and back-down, invitation and studied contempt. Muttered curses, unuttered racial slurs, and deepening resentments follow. There is movement and avoidance, a dispute that could spiral dodged one

11

more time, until the next one. This could arise in the crowded city, in the surly neighborhood, in the watchful workplace, or in the most innocuous of circumstances. Here is the disdain for social order and social standards with road rage, public urination, and growing discourtesies part of the edgy counterculture of defiance and disregard. Together, they form an extended racial middle finger stuck in the face.

Next, there is the obscenity of political and institutionalized corruption, criminal conduct at an already towering, monumental level. It continues to widen and lengthen. Nothing splits the races apart more than this monster. Black people strongly believe that an Indian government runs amok and steals the nation blind. They believe that Indians tacitly support this blatant criminality with their votes, prospers from it through their presence and color, and resists exposure and justice through their silence and intransigence. On the other hand, Indians see this same issue as sometimes overblown, not physically harmful, and not so different from what was the practice during the Black PNC administrations. Unsurprisingly, the anger and disagreement nurtured by each group for the other grows geometrically with each passing day, and each new unresolved exposure. Exposures to the tune of tens of millions of dollars, sometimes hundreds of millions, and which the Black Man believes work to his own severe disadvantage and social retardation.

These are only three areas, each of which will be explored in more detail later; but this is the prevailing mindset, where the all-enveloping, all-consuming factor of race cannot fade into a wished for state of irrelevancy and immateriality. Not when it has come to represent and signify so much. It cannot be for peoples so self-indoctrinated; for political operators so unceasingly manipulative; or for an environment that is so ready to embrace the worst that is spawned, inculcated, and nurtured. This is the steamy environment where contemplations are veined with visions of growing rifts and approaching cataclysm. No one knows when or how; or by whose hand. Just that it is inevitable, as the current situation and political arrangements cannot stand, cannot continue, cannot endure.

12

CHAPTER II

TO SAY OR NOT TO SAY: THE PARAMOUNTCY OF RACE

"Here I stand, I cannot do otherwise."
-Martin Luther

It is a taboo subject to some extent for most. It reduces people to the uneasy, the untruthful, and the unspoken. Guyanese are no exception in this regard. Genuine thoughts, feelings and positions on this most unpalatable of subjects are only shared within the deep, secret confines of families. There may be some lowering of the guard and candor in the company of close friends, trusted colleagues, and longstanding neighbors. But only with those of the same racial ancestry is there full-fledged frankness and daring openness on the issues, controversies, and conflicts encompassed by race relations in Guyana. Of course, if there is a hard difference between individuals from the major races, then the concealed bile and venom can trample all civility in the ugliest of forms. It has to be seen and heard to be believed, but it is well-known.

Two Taboo Subjects –and then a Third One

It is just as well-known that in numerous homes in the Guyana of the past, there were two subjects that governing adults declared as off-limits and not open for discussion. They were religion and politics. Today, many still retreat from any close grappling with these two problematic, controversial subjects, and limit themselves to careful, half-hearted ventures into the believed acrimonious waters. A few hardy souls, some under the protection of anonymity, have grown comfortable in accessing the print and electronic media to express opinions and cross swords with others on political matters, as they exist in Guyana. While politics enmeshes race in this country, race is still something of a sacred cow, an untouchable area for thoughtful, honest, and purposeful public engagement. There are occasional references, fleeting skirmishes, and choreographed postures; but there has been no determined, principled effort to strip this particular cow of sacred skin or sinew, and to face the realities of local existence, as they really are. No, let there be none of that. What good would come out of broadcasting the national family secret?

To be sure, there is legitimate concern-even fear-that such activity could lead to malicious conduct, extreme views, offensive expression, and deterioration into ugliness; that it could produce more unsettling questions than constructive answers. This is regrettable. The result has been that this most sensitive, most volatile, most divisive, yet most relevant national conversation is comatose, even dead before arrival. To the detriment of this nation and its peoples, discussion of race is a nonstarter that is best hidden away and left to run wherever it might in the closeted circles and barricaded minds of the riven national house.

Without a doubt, the time has come for us to look at one another in the eye. And for the first time, let the mask be peeled away; let the truth be told; and let the soul be bared at the core to-and for-each other. It is way past the time for Guyanese to acknowledge the workings of the mind, and the way the heart beats in order to examine and to understand. Let the collective soul be exposed, so that this nation can see to its face what lurks in its craw and gut; and in its sleep.

Race –The Alpha and Omega of Guyanese Existence

Race –differences, awareness, relations –is the beginning, end, and thereafter of life in Guyana. It fills daily existence in a multiplicity of ways small and large, sometimes subconsciously, mostly unexpressed. Race resonates in the commerce, across the fence, and beyond the boundary of Guyanese with all the tumult of a tree crashing in the forest. It is a tree that disturbs and displaces much in its passage; the difference is that its fall is heard and seen and anticipated every time. It never fails to shake the local ground.

In city and office, village and home, thoroughfare and glare of the day, there is much of the unuttered, and the not so invisible to give pause. Even to alarm. It could be a look, a steady stare, an impatient frown; or just the coolness of silence and space wherever the place may be. It might be the jostling for the first to go at blinking traffic lights in a busy intersection; failure to yield; or the don't-give-a-damn arrogance of parking wherever it pleases that inhibits movement in a town that grows more cramped by the day. It might be the selection of a vendor in the marketplace to make a weekly purchase of greens and vegetables; or the believed discriminatory pricing (or manufactured shortage) applied by seller to buyer. Then again, it just might be the mayhem at the bus parks that is the pungent essence of commuters' daily travails and existence.

Three contexts out of the numerous interactions experienced and endured routinely; three ordinary contexts that gyrate the internal spirit level of taut beliefs and lurking hypersensitivity. Three public contexts-three only-that confirm what is blindly, reflexively believed about the next person from the other side. Namely that "is suh deh stay; deh caan change." Or "all deh want is fuh deh pun tap." Or "dah is why ah doan waan nuthin fuh duh wit dem; ah hate dem."

This is representative of the daily, hourly, perpetual face-off, flare-up, and sizzle out that graces the Guyanese day, and that is part and parcel of the uneasy chemistry of the races. It is suppressed most of the time, but it lingers all the time. This is the world of Black and Indian citizens, as they commingle in business places, in public places, in private vehicles, in lonely streets. It is a stiff, guarded minuet relived day after day. In some ways, it is like two dogs meeting by chance for the first time. Watch as

15

they circle and size up each other, before parting company and going their individual ways; sometimes they growl menacingly and flash teeth. Unlike the canines, the humans wall themselves off in moving silos; and like the dogs, they are sometimes careful and measuring, other times jarringly aggressive, and on occasion prone to ugly eruption. At the massed street level, this would be profanity laced, and racially offensive. In no time, the atmosphere becomes charged; people avert their eyes; others hurry away; some stand ready to pour fuel on the fire; more than a few wait expectantly –either loudly or quietly.

Such situations fade at their own pace; but they represent more incendiary fragments in the growing stockpile of live, and not forgotten, racial animosities. This makes it ever so easy to resurrect rapidly for other occasions involving disagreements between other members of the two races. Or in the run-up and aftermath of elections. Embers do not extinguish; they stay warm, they flare and burn all the time.

This is the poison at the heart of the two major races in Guyana; and it infects onlookers, neighbors, and strangers. A mob of one, an ordinary dispute involving two, can quickly escalate into partitioning along racial lines. There follows the taking of sides ignorantly, but out of blind racial loyalty; the venting of old generalized hostilities; the recording of more confirmation of the way the other side can be unfailingly unjust, unreasonable, and uncivilized. The finger pointing never stops, the blame game is shrill and unceasing; and self-examination is an alien consideration. This is the raw teeming reality of the streets, where there is a premium on studied avoidance, and cautious distance amidst the just-below-the-surface racial acids.

There is just too much history, distrust and discontent wrapped in these expressions and episodes of the moment, too much hostility trapped in the heat of the day for things to be otherwise. How many of such pregnant confrontations are part of a regular day? How long can this continue to hold in forced confinement? How long will one race soar, while the other sinks?

There might be an Amin watching and thinking, and not liking things as they are. Or there could be a Jerry Rawlins lurking in the breast of a rash, impatient citizen somewhere. A citizen sufficiently disgusted, appalled, and infuriated at the plight of this society to abandon caution and seize matters in his own hands in an attempt to right wrongs; to reverse the field; and to distribute hope. How long will Guyanese style democracy prevail where the few are enriched at the expense of the many? It is the same few who are seen as hailing from mainly one race today; and which was the same sad story before, but with a different color. It was Richard Nixon who said that *"A politician knows that the best way to be a winner is to make the other side feel it does not have to be a loser."* In Guyana, such a stance falls on rocky soil and dies an immediate death; it has no place to go or to grow. Further, it has never been tried, and induces mirth, if not scornful dismissal. This is how reckless the leaders have been.

Thus, from home to street, on land and in the air, and whether in the big City or remote village, the wellspring of perceptions, the flood of expectations, and rain of denunciations are part of the same shabby continuum. It is a continuum bounded by political calculation, ethnic fears, and group hatreds. The driving force, the Holy Grail is power; power at all costs, by any tawdry means necessary, and to monopolize it for self. There is this steadfast determination to hold on to power, to not relinquish an inch, to control and manipulate society, and to play sinister games with the lives of many. Some like it this way, none more so than those entrenched in the bastions of power. They lie, they cheat, they steal, they divide, and they laugh in the faces of the people, especially the poor and the Black. There are no longer subtle or careful —only recklessly contemptuous.

PART II

The People and the Politics: Raw
Emotions, Naked Passions

CHAPTER III

The PPP ~ A Catalogue of Racial Instigation, Injustice, and Injury

"Government, even in its best state is a necessary evil; in its worse state, an intolerable one."
-Thomas Paine

What is this monstrosity? From where did this fiendish beast come?

Once, the PPP was supposedly the party of the unrepresented poor, the voiceless working class, the unorganized grassroots, the struggling masses. At best, that might have been the hazy untested reality once upon a time, a long time ago. At worst, it is one more myth, another cruel hoax played upon the afflicted in Guyana. The truth is closely intertwined with the hoax. Because this political apparition has long abandoned many of the things and peoples it was supposed to have championed. Nowadays, the PPP is about insinuation and instigation through use of the race card, and the personal profits resulting therefrom; about self-preservation above all other considerations; and about racial injustice and injury that seeks to pummel Black Guyanese into submission. The party's words, postures, actions, and visions are intended to separate, and represent a preponderance of perversities. They incite. They alarm.

Insinuation and Instigation –The race card

Today, in this its second lease on political life, the PPP has enthusiastically forsworn most of its trumpeted values; it has reconstructed itself into an unrecognizable monster. Like a Komodo dragon, its very breath is toxic, its touch injurious. Hence, the bottom-house seminars and community summit conferences, as spearheaded by visiting PPP stalwarts-some of cabinet rank-have certain common and sharp ingredients focused on racial segmentation: There is manufactured tension, sharp urgency, and surging anxieties. In one Indian community after another, trusted PPP agents deliver a fixed script that massages the heart and stiffens the resolve, especially of the wavering and the questioning. It starts with the poisoned chalice of the script, which is frightening-as is intended-with its febrile promises of failure and fall, and the waiting damnation of racial hell, which grinds the frightened into abject compliance. It goes like this.

"Ayuh playin wit trouble" "Stap de foolishness or ayuh gun see fair-play an' duh ain guh be nice." "Wha is it ayuh waan fuh see?" Ayuh want fuh see dem Black man geh bak in power?" "Like ayuh fuget wha used to happen …" These are a snapshot of the blunt verbal hatchet blows delivered in person by party veterans and emissaries, who wrap themselves in seriousness that is intended to induce panic and fear. It is reported that one of the PPP nobility went so far as to say that if the PNC got back in power personal suicide would follow. This is to shore up nervous Indian loyalists, and to squeeze the wavering into line –the voting line. In this torrent of torment, this pressurized environment, what is a pliant Indian to do? He is conflicted, made weak, and fearful. Man and woman, and parent and worker worry about the security of their homes, of their persons; the honor of daughters; the hope of progress; and the multiple threats of intimidation, crime, and violence. All of these visceral fears, these perennial worries are scratched and deeply speared. There can be only one response. The fence sitters and critical-if any-are overwhelmed and swept away, as political racial bonding tightens. This is the shameless racial insinuation and instigation, of a clandestine kind, practiced at the individual and residential level, and in the political strongholds. It is crass, calculating, and coercive. The bottom line is this: This strategy of mind games and fear mongering yields the desired results. Every time.

All of this is underground, out-of-sight, and out of earshot. Or so it is believed. But were not these same political threats, this line of appeal-along with the accompanying physical flinch and emotional fear-solidly incorporated in a very furious public outburst that followed the November, 2011 general elections? What was heard was the equivalent of: If Indians play games with voting rights, they will get burned with individual rights, and they will be made to pay through loss of racial rights. According to this bellicose, apprentice party leader, some Indian voters played such a game by staying away from the polls and sitting on their hands. Now they will pay; all Indians will pay. They will learn the hard way, as they have failed to live up to their obligation (yes, obligation) to go out and vote for the PPP, the Indian party. This was the message from this callow Red Guard from the Guyanese bush, as he flagellated his betters. Embedded in this revealing diatribe was the ominous promise of the Black party's rollback of what was present, of Indian gains. No race or color was mentioned; none was needed. All the old ghosts and bogeymen were exhumed and placed on full public display in this naked racial dress-down; there was scant disregard for the wider implications and reach of the words uttered; of how they could be interpreted. It was Indian consumption and Indian absorption day, and it was not at a bottom house, but a public in-the-face obscenity. Now if this was not divisive, then nothing is; if it was not naked and ugly and revealing, then all is well. And there is only the healing and harmonious in this land, and between the races. But the reality is terribly different, isn't it?

During all of this rounding up and corralling of racially treasonous Indians who had strayed off the voting reservation, Black leaders and the Black segment of the population listened and observed with keen interest at this flash of political pornography. They looked on approvingly at thinking, conscientious Indians expressing their anger and dismay at the daily barbarisms, and at what had become acceptable norms; they heard the excoriations and beat-down directed at the denominator of race and the perpetuation of racial exclusivism; they relived 'Apaan jaat' this time with 21ˢᵗ Century subtitles, and in full color. It was petulant, it was shrill, it was jagged. It was reminiscent of the former abuser-in-chief and champion of the cuss-down. But who cares —message delivered. It had all the subtle power of insinuation and instigation delivered in bold swift strokes and apoplectic flourish. AND IT WAS ALL ABOUT RACE AND BLIND RACIAL ALLEGIANCE.

What was the rowel goading spokespeople to such extremes of posture? Why the desperation of spirit and degeneration of vocabulary?

Self-Preservation and Self-Perpetuation -Power

Once, the PPP was thought to be pure and innocent. Not anymore. It has lost its way, and has no interest in returning to what it might have been. It does not care about how it is seen, its sordid record, its accumulation of ills and degeneracy. All it cares about is self-preservation and self-perpetuation. It is why rebellious stay-at-home Indians, who spoke in clear, unequivocal terms, were publicly flogged for failing to deliver their voting birthright to the crooked cabal. Part of the party's fear is about the Black opposition returning to power, but there is more.

The name of the game is power. The focus is on how to remain in power come what may, and on the backs of gullible docile supporters; there is no interest in doing what is right or fair; what circumstances demand in this ruptured society. The hardline men and women in the PPP could learn from that artful political dodger Richard Nixon who counseled: *"A politician knows that only if he leaves room for discussion and room for concession can he gain room to maneuver."* Instead, the party is obsessed with the reach and rewards of near absolute power, including the dark side of its exercise; it will go to any lengths to stave off a loss of power for that promises fateful consequences for many of its leading lights. Thus, it will use the race card and the hegemony afforded by numbers to poison its believers with race hatreds and powerful fears; it will instigate circumstances that fuel racial distrust and deeper division. And while doing so, it will spew its copyrighted lyrics about unity and nationhood, as huge sections of this country smolder and stir restlessly. It does so knowingly.

Staying in power is mandatory. While there is unimagined greed and lust for riches, the party has to maintain its hold on power or dire calamities are promised. Should there be a successor government that is halfway viable and only partially principled, then discovery, exposure, asset seizure, public humiliation, and imprisonment are some of the perils in store for PPP

powers and cronies. It is why out of reflexive routine, and sometimes desperation, the party resorts to the race card to set matters on the right track,
to maintain the status quo and the gravy train. It must secure itself first;
this includes family, friends and the favored few; these are overwhelmingly
Indian. At no time, it should be said are cleanup operations considered,
which would have been the reaction of any principled patriotic party. Sure
it is an undertaking Augean in scope, and formidable in the mere contem-
plation, for there are just too many party stalwarts and too much money
involved. Still, that should have been the rational response; let the chips
fall. Instead, there was this ruckus laden post-election explosion. Why?

Because too much is at stake: the palaces, the visible trophies of inexplicable wealth, the invisible bloated bank holdings, the lavish lifestyles,
and the trail of dirty money and chronic thievery. No one is fooled by sub-
missions of family generosity, overseas largesse, sham investigations, and
temporary resignations; they are farcical on the face of things, lack any substance, and are intended to misrepresent and mislead. Then, there are all
those suspicious, mysterious, extrajudicial, national security related killings
from a few years back. Clearly, it is all about self-preservation, of denying
the reach of the law; of subverting justice; and of protecting the closed circle
of kith and kin. To hell with everybody else; if the PPP does not care about
rank-and-file Indians, why should it care about the welfare of Black people?

The party and its still thinking people know that astute (and
street smart) citizens see through the charade; they know, too, that it
is only a matter of time when not-so-random sparks-racially fissionable
sparks-mushroom into the local equivalent of a nuclear detonation. And it
would be because of the underlying racial volatility, the strangling discontent, and the searing anger that singes the eyeballs of the people, mainly
of one kind.

Chew on this: if people can be killed wantonly to assure the upper hand
in power struggles, then what is a little toying with the race card, with
using the Indian voter? It serves its purpose, doesn't it? And who cares
about racial injustice and injury? After all, such are the spoils of war. And
this is war, let there be no mistake. It is why Babu John, that most sacred
of PPP and Indian shrines dedicated to the memory of the party's martyrs
and saints, is the cleverly chosen place for the annual racial saber-rattling
delivered through coarse full-fledged harangues, and not so coded racial

messages to the faithful. Listen and hear, then spread the word! It never fails to instill fear and loathing in captive Indian devotees; especially when they hear about "hate" and "haters." All of this stokes the apprehensions and oppression endured by Black Guyanese.

Racial Injustice and Injury –The politics of oppression

The PPP has become what the PNC represented during its extended tenure, which ended some two decades ago. Then Indians disappeared from public presence and significance; today the Black man is nowhere in sight much along the same lines. In all candor, and in homage to accuracy, it can be said that the PPP first walked in the footsteps of the PNC, and now has surpassed it in racial attitudes, racial postures, and racial conduct. It can be more nuanced when the occasion demands, but is no less devastating in terms of injury, indignity, and injustice meted out to Black Guyanese. If anything, it is more devastating.

Recently much has been said by many-including PPP supporters-that an earlier leader was crude and boorish, and someone lacking in simple courtesy and everyday decency. The problem is that, while there is now some absence of the churlishness and meanness, all the old failed policies and approaches continue uninterrupted, and severely impacts the welfare and vision of the local Black populace. The party persists in doing the barest minimum-and under duress only-for unifying and solidifying this society into a cohesive, refreshing newness. It ignores to its own peril, and that of its supporters, this commonsense statement from John F. Kennedy: *"If a free society cannot help the many who are poor, it cannot save the few who are rich."* The PPP will not listen; it is too consumed with itself to care, to do something different, something meaningful. No! Action in such directions would dilute spoils, diminish power, and lead to accountability. Therefore, there is this master-servant (boss and boy) relationship, and lord-serf mentality that orders the times and relations between governing party and citizens.

Consider the following abbreviated composite. It is a mouthful of cardboard, and a stomach full of acid, which pulverizes the gut and inflames the brain. That is, Black ones.

First, there is the bureaucratic; to say that no blood is shed would be an inaccuracy–the draining effects are the same. There is the insult of senior Black public servants subjected to the indignity of perpetual acting appointments; they are of the wrong color and in the wrong place at the wrong time. There is the public pronouncement that Black Foreign Service talent in Guyana is noticeably absent; this had to be doubly wounding coming from the ruling party's chief spokesman, himself a Black man of considerable talents. These are talents utilized by his Indian brethren to move heavy loads and execute dirty jobs. He can handle all of the unwanted chores, but is not good enough-trusted enough-to lead those for whom he has done so much. There is the cronyism and cratered playing field, which effectively locks out the Black contractor and entrepreneur. In a nutshell, the Black public servant cannot get near the job, and the Black businessman cannot be part of the contract bonanza. The prestige and money are off-limits to each; and so Black Guyanese exist like unrecognized islands on the margins, which are left unattended and kept firmly separated from the mainland of action and advancement. None of this is a source of contentment or good feeling for Black people left out in the cold. Rather, each is seen as one more example of disrespect, injustice, and injury. They accumulate, and with each the sinews of anger enlarge and harden.

So far, this is with regard to those marginalized and steadfastly ignored in the offices and temples of the moneychangers. The so-called bloodless side of things, it is the business side of a spreading, crippling attrition. Now, it is time for a quick introductory look at where matters are dark and bloody and sometimes lethal. Where to make a start?

To begin with, there are the dirty tricks men within the bowels of the PPP hierarchy who recruit Black thugs to harass, intimidate, and unleash violence against Indian pedestrians and businesses during opposition arranged protest marches and demonstrations. The Black opposition and its supporters are immediately demonized. (*More coverage is in the following chapter*).

There is rage at the criminalization of their men, and the numerous killings in the name of National Security, and selective crime prevention. Black Guyanese are incensed over the lack of official action and any justice when there are obvious executions of Black men in the street by the police in highly suspect circumstances. There is the indignity of being forced to beg first, then agitate vociferously, for some speck of justice. There is the humiliation of paternalism and charity, of having to line-up and wait for political crumbs. They simmer. They rail at the demonization that disrespects and insults from Black leaders to Black losers. So whether jobs, crime, contracts, equitable distribution, racial bias, racial targeting, or state violence, it is the unshakeable belief of Black Guyanese that they have been subject to systematic discrimination, and are lesser for all of this. Lesser individually, and lesser as a people. In Guyanese parlance, all of this represents the heaping of more coals in an already crowded, smoking coal pot.

The assaults on Black dignity and being rarely stop. They are at varying times subtle, in-your-face, creeping, or relentless. From a Black perspective, this is demeaning and makes their existence an endless agony, an ongoing nightmare. Each dreary day, each irrefutable example, each sharp recollection, each powerful perception, each wrathful conversation adds one more degree to their torture chamber that is Guyana. Indians should know this – they were there as a people, some still live this way today as individuals and communities, and none more so than the poor. Black people are infuriated at their lot, the hopelessness, at what they have been reduced to, and where they find themselves. There is still more, and it has to do with control.

The Old Communistic Obsession with Control

The PPP is obsessed with control. It must know everything, respond to each item of criticism, and impose a sleazy presence in almost all spheres of activity in Guyana. It takes umbrage at any questioning of its record from any source; but that umbrage is never more obvious and vehement than when the source is an Indian voice or pen that points to its malefic record on race relations, and the deplorable, dangerous state of such affairs as it exists currently. It will attack (using every available channel) those messengers of inconvenient racial truths. Significant Black contributors are so disgusted, so furious, that they have simply withdrawn from any public engagement. In and of itself, this is ominous. But the PPP pays no heed; it giggles.

The party has to be present anywhere there is the potential to challenge the regime; it has a ready battalion of fawning, ambitious, craven men and women who will do anything to get ahead, to position themselves for a piece of the lucrative action. Therefore, it must infiltrate, dilute, divide, and compromise any actual or potential opposition to its rule. This includes such diverse areas as trade unions, the media, the University, the army, the police force, anti-corruption institutions, PNC strongholds, and the PNC itself (repeat, the PNC itself!), among other spaces. It will first invade these areas, and then undermine them; it must have its ear through its own people in every group, particularly those that have the potential to develop into something substantial and threatening. When concerned Guyanese take the time and interest to look more closely at some of these domestic bodies, they easily see the slimy and putrid hand of a party dedicated to its own self-perpetuation through presence and control. There is nothing healthy or wholesome for the country and to bind its peoples.

Most of this is traceable to its communist pedigree which insists on the need to know; and to an irrational paranoia, when the party thinks that it doesn't know enough and something is brewing. It knows of nothing else. It sees enemies in every shadow, and fatal menace in every syllable; no one can be allowed to peer, even for a moment, into the conduct of the local Kremlinologists. Aside from the deep-seated ideological roots, the PPP cannot afford to be anything but totalitarian, even tyrannical; given its now long sordid history of knavery best encapsulated in financial killings, and plain regular killings. The last word is that there are too many ugly secrets, so there are wide swaths of territory to cover and control, so as to ensure that Black people are kept in their place at the bottom. This is where they belong; this is where they must stay. Thus, the party is everywhere in some surreptitious, insidious form.

The party must distribute its version of truth and play its mind games in Black communities, such as Linden. It awards broadcast permission to friends who are sure to use such facilities to spread the party line to shape public opinion; it severely limits similar availability to others who are outside of its circle, and that means the doldrums of Black suffocation; its people invade the Internet, blogs, and newspaper columns, to taint discussions, to make them dishonest and sleazy. It is all about control and thought suppression, through the propagation of the PPP mindset. This usually means an Indian voice, an Indian presence, and an Indian pen.

These actions are, however viewed, inimical and destructive to progress in this society. Given the political origins and angles-whether subtle or blatant-of the skullduggery, there inevitably develops and festers the hard racial suspicions, if not heavy prejudice, within large segments of the population to the detriment of one and all. In plainer language, and from a Black way of thinking, the Indian party first oppresses, and then seeks to control the Black man. It tells him how he should think, what he should say, and who should say it. It pressures him to listen and view those whom he despises. Last, it dangles him in the wind.

To facilitate all of this, there is this expensive, intricate, deleterious propaganda machinery that is in constant, furious motion. Huge sums are spent-gifted to the favored-to sing the party's praises, defend its unmasked villains, and savage its critics. As an aside, the new president, in a slice of verbal buffoonery, called the premeditated gifts of precious broadcast licenses to favored operators and opportunists "commitments" made by his predecessor; this is the idea of both leaders of what social and racial democracy represent. This omnipresent machinery is devoted to imploring and pressing the Indian fence sitters to come back to the racial house; to cajoling the weak, the greedy, the needy, the corrupt, and the self-centered to come forward and share in the free money floating around; and to look-ing for new takers, including Black takers. There is always a position (and money) for those collaborators willing to sell themselves, their community, and their brother to get up, to be recognized, and to be rewarded. A few have yielded to the inducements. Of course, this incurs the flaming wrath of the hardy faithful left behind to sacrifice and struggle. Further, the bit-terness calcifies, given the associated racial contours and contexts usually associated with these political manipulations and maneuvers.

Yes, this is what the onetime embodiment of individual and collective aspirations has metabolized into: a national yoke and abomination, and a source of regional derision. As many struggle and starve daily, the PPP remains immovably focused on dominance of every aspect of Guyanese life, and for its own advancement. Its racial chemists and witchdoctors are adept at fanning the flames of fear and tension; at pushing the right buttons with the right people to goad the uncertain into action through "Ah yuh waan dem black maan tek over again?" And "Ah yuh fuget wha happen in McKenzie and Wismar and Buxton?" This puts a gloss on the crudity that takes root and flourishes from bottom house to Babu John. Along the way, it tramps on muffled treacherous feet starting at Freedom House, before flitting across the length and breadth of village and region, inclusive of wedding house, religious house, outhouse, penthouse, whorehouse, and dead house. Thus a country is inundated, and is enfeebled; thus it is destroyed by the poisons within and from above. For the uncertain with their newfound, fragile consciences, who are a little less trusting, and more resistant, a special steel-toed, steroid powered kick is reserved in the form of: "See wha happen in Linden? Deh only leh de own peeple paas. All deh kno fuh do is bun." And for those who need that extra torque of persuasion applied, "See who get raab and beat up in Agricola?"

This is a compressed version of the PPP at work and in full flow, of the divisive nature of its triumph and rule, of the harm that it inflicts, and of the fear and rage it excites. This does not bode well for the well-being of this society, be it harmonious relationship, be it national togetherness, be it lasting peace. Sooner or later, there will be a day of reckoning.

CHAPTER IV

BLACK FEAR, BLACK RAGE

*"We have petitioned; we have remonstrated; we have supplicated ...
Our petitions have been slighted, our remonstrations have produced
additional violence and insult; our supplications have been disregarded ..."*
-Patrick Henry

I am not aware. I am not aware. I am not aware. The speaker did not say "damn it" or "damn you." But he might have come close in his mind. This was the continuing one man chorus, as sung by a minister of the government, before the Commission of Inquiry into the Linden killings.

I don't recall. I don't recall. I don't.... And this was the nucleus of the testimony-some might rightly call it non-testimony-of a senior police officer on the ground at Linden during the killings when his turn came before the same Commission of Inquiry. Everyone who paraded before the commissioners swore to tell the truth. Few did; from all appearances, most didn't. Still, the crux of the story remains: Shots were fired, people were killed. AND NOBODY KNOWS ANYTHING. Or more accurately, no one of any stature-whether through direct official responsibility or broad oversight-knows or remembers anything.

By the same token, it is expected-perhaps decreed-that Black Guyanese also should not be aware, not recall, and be conveniently oblivious to the sordid and horrendous accumulation of injustices and indignities that have been their lot for the last two decades. As individuals and groups and communities of their segment of the population groan under the increasingly crushing weight of burden after burden, as they reel from political atrocity, as they stumble from the multiple hammer blows of non-representation, loss of hope, and mounting despair, Black Guyanese are all pushed, encouraged, and expected to do just what the two witnesses did. That is: THEY MUST FORGET! THEY MUST PRETEND! THEY MUST SUBMIT. THEY MUST MOVE ON!

To restate the obvious, this is a lot of poisoned razor-grass territory to cover unclothed. Hence, it is appropriate to take a careful look at what is expected (demanded) that they ignore and forget. Simultaneously, Black citizens must question themselves as to whether they could and should. Power-or lack of power-is a good enough place to start. It might be the best place of all; since it opens the first door and showcases the stage of numerous political barbarisms.

An Invisible, Inconsequential Presence

Black people have no real political power in Guyana. In addition, they have minimal economic power. Last, they have a passing social presence, one that amounts to the window dressing of numbers. While the Black political opposition, and the wider joint opposition, is SOMETIMES duly recognized, Black people are not properly seated at the table of deliberation and decision making. Black people desire with a burning passion to take their RIGHTFUL place at this table. The Black man unwaveringly believes that he has earned that right-is due that place of authority and power-through the blood and bodies of his ancestors and martyrs, which cry out from the stained soil of a savage history.

They, through their representatives, might be in the room, but they are at the far end of the conference room; they might even be in the second tier or outer ring of attendees. There they are: mostly inaudible for they are not listened to; mainly invisible because they are not acknowledged; and practically inconsequential for all the difference they make. However examined, this is the bottom line: They have no place, they have no say, they have no sway. They are reduced to an irrelevancy on the immense issues of the day that impact this nation and their own lives, mostly negatively. Here are some supporting positions.

First, budgetary slashes and pressures are introduced in 2012, as a means of holding the government's feet to the fire for responsibility and accountability. What is the PPP government's response? It ignores and circumvents the restrictions imposed by discovering and utilizing funds from other sources. Creative, perhaps, but this is the equivalent of urinating upon the financial handcuffs and straightjackets introduced. They are rendered meaningless.

It has been the same story of determined derailing and dismissing when bills that ran the parliamentary gantlet go to the president for assent. After all the strenuous efforts involving bickering and hollering and cursing, there is the brick wall of presidential non-assent. The governing party is sharp enough to foresee that, if enacted into law, there would be a lessening of its Stalinist stranglehold on society. Thus, there is the bleak reality of efforts reduced to the grand total of zero. What is there of substance to show after a year of "New Dispensation?"

Third, most-if not all-opposition inquiries and demands in the National Assembly for important documents are stymied and stonewalled, if not outright rejected. Whether related to NICIL procedures and activities, or expensive projects, or secret deals, the opposition might as well not be there, not have asked. SCREW ALL OF YOU! GET OUT OF HERE! GET LOST! Clearly, the much heralded "New Dispensation" is more of the same old shabby, worm infested story of the last ten to fifteen years. There is no difference, for nothing is new under the Guyanese political sun. The arrogance and contempt (and guile) continues unabated.

In sum, the preceding snapshots present a composite of the innovative, the disingenuous, and the arguably illegitimate. This is what is thought of the opposition, how it is neutralized. These are just a handful of examples that illuminate the impotency of the opposition and, by extension, those whom they represent.

Some questions arise: Where is the presence and influence of Black Guyanese, when the government spits continuously in the faces of its leaders? What is the meaning of their vote when the decisions of their elected representatives are lateraled to the courts and the final judgment of unelected arbiters? How are they contributing when there is so much indifference and indignity? They might as well not be here, or there, or anywhere. The problem is that they are here; and their anger is increasing, as their patience is decreasing with every new example of disregard and disrespect in these demonstrations of democracy in action. Indignity and injustice festers. They breed resentment, stiffen the spine, and harden the heart.

Whether real or perceived, imagined or instigated, accurate or exaggerated, indignity and injustice inflate the local racial volcano. Like a volcano, strength is gathered, and there is heaving and partial venting on occasion. The restless stirring grows as the record and continuum of government excesses and obscenities mount against more and more Black victims. Black citizens count, they rage, they remember ....

Accumulated Memories of Countless Outrages: Inequity First

They remember the insults and humiliations mentioned before of acting appointments in what is left of the traditional public service, now decimated; of the embarrassments foisted upon mainly Black workers and their unions, with the latter now effectively castrated. They look at the old public service and wonder where it disappeared so quickly, and rage at what has replaced it at multiples of the original cost. Meaning that there is the regiment strength cohort of highly compensated contract workers, who are mainly non-Black. It is some of these same contract beneficiaries-a goodly number-who then turn right around and gouge the public daily through their involvement in an endless series of corrupt activities.

Yes, Black Guyanese see and remember a public service gutted of significant Black employees, and learn of a Foreign Service devoid of Black professionals, but filled with a dismal roll of party mediocrities, and chronic lawbreakers. The reason advanced for the void in the diplomatic corps was startling: There is an insufficiency of appropriately qualified Black people to serve in these roles. Somehow, and in short order a handful of Black names and faces were located to remedy an egregious situation, characterized by the injury of denial, and followed by insult of lack of qualifications, skills, and competencies. Where does it stop? And how long will these and other "eye-pass" be permitted to continued unaddressed and unresolved?

The fire is further fueled. It is fueled through the shabby treatment of one of the linchpins in any society —teachers. Like the public service, there is discontent with pay, working conditions, and work benefits. Plus there is the deep seated resentment that intensifies year after year, as exemplified in the unilateral, high-handed, lowdown, dismissive single digit wage increases, which are literally stuffed into the pockets of union and recipients in the form of "it has to be taken, whether liked or not." There is no choice; there are no alternatives. This approach was perfected by the PPP government in its stormy dealings with the old public service; it has now become the norm of negotiations with groups dominated by Black workers. While this stream of Guyanese is handled cheaply and with disdain, there is patience, respect, and generosity where the workers and recruits are Indian. Thus bauxite workers and Linden come up short against sugar and Berbice, while non-contract Black workers lose out every time against their contracted Indian counterparts who are smothered in money.

This disrespectful, uneven, inequitable treatment of the public service and the teaching profession-known opposition bastions, and heavily populated by Black Guyanese-stands in stark contrast to the government's interest and heavy financial subsidization of the problematic sugar industry. For a certainty, sugar equals a predominantly Indian presence, which translates to votes from an immovable PPP stronghold. This is all well and good, until the issue of equity is broached. Why the patent disparity? Why the obvious in-your-face double standard? Where is the economic and racial democracy? Why not some movement towards spreading the wealth and narrowing the gap and sowing goodwill? Why the denials of all these realities?

In all of these areas, Black losers-more rightly than wrongly-form their own opinions and conclusions. Inevitably, they settle at the rocky storm-lashed square of politics, power and RACE. This leads to the pervasive disillusionment-and related anger-of losing ground, disappearing stature, nonexistent status, nowhere to go, nothing to hope for, and nothing to do. They do not want to hear about democracy and freedom; they seek to feed their families, live with dignity, and feature in the national power calculus.

This is rejected out-of-hand at every turn and every opportunity, however. From the PPP's absolutist perspective, there is no room for compromise; there is no need to accommodate. At least not yet; or not until the full force of reactionary circumstances in the sharpness of time compel an involuntary adjustment of these squalid racial strategies and tactics, and the arrival of suddenly discovered willingness. That reactionary force promises to come, and to shape the willingness to adjust and accommodate.

Thus far, the fast moving instances of Black discontent and disenchantment have focused on segments in the occupational and economic spheres. But there is a darker, even more roiling side to the fear and anger of Black Guyanese. It is ugly, it is criminal, and it is reprehensible. What follows next is dirty and searing. For a certainty, there are active Black participants in this sullied environment, but Black people also live (and die) with the brunt of the consequences. They pay harsh bitter prices. They pay in lost blood, lost lives, lost opportunities, and lost potential. And just plain losing all around. Most of this can be traced to roots in the narcotics trade, which just might be the preeminent industry in this country.

Narcotics Related Atrocities Next

The narcotics industry employs Black males as transporters, protectors, enforcers, and executioners. It does nothing for racial understanding and harmony in Guyana, when it is widely known and accepted that the major employers and shot-callers in this evil trade are mainly Indians. To pour more vinegar into open sores, these same Indian kingpins are strongly perceived-immovably so-to be the beneficiaries of ironclad protection from an Indian government. And which, in turn, was defended by a phantom strike force assembled and unleashed by these same Indian narcotics tycoons, among others. A phantom force, it must be said, made up of primarily Black shooters, and which ended up killing mainly Black men. This is believed as gospel by those with ear to the ground, and who possess mere smidgens of street sense and awareness. Now is this incendiary by itself or not? A situation where Indian men employ Black men to do dirty work-political work-through killing Black men? Leaving aside for a moment, the political elements and objectives, this is, in and of itself, racial napalm. Plain and simple, and just as undeniable.

Just as plain, and no less incendiary, is the parade of Black drug mules hauled before the courts, who readily plead guilty for the routine sentence and slap of four years in jail. It should be said that some in society entertain serious doubts, as to whether these sentences are served in any great portion, or served at all. That is, incentivizing arrangements can be made to induce early-very early-freedom from the penal system. That is bad enough, but the bigger issue that burns is this: the minnows are occasionally snared and publicly displayed as examples of a functioning narcotics-judicial-penal complex, where justice is handed down, **when it is anything but so.** While the "big fish" remain insulated, coddled, and get away scot-free all the time. AND THEY ARE MAINLY INDIANS. It must be made clear that there are Black drug kingpins on the local scene, but they pale into numbers, significance, and power when arrayed alongside their Indian brothers-in-crime.

These are the same narcotics and money laundering characters that have used their overflowing cash machines to distort the skyline and commandeer the sidewalks of the capital city, Georgetown. The countryside displays its own celebrations of the dirty money rush. The PPP broadcast apparatus calls it business and progress, with the most shameless of countenances. It is the same twin evils of narcotics and money laundering that have transformed-and keep transforming-a once largely non-Indian rectangle, Georgetown, into a mainly Indian industrial and commercial swamp.

Additionally, more wickedly, it is the some of the same narcotics product that is reported to be delivered by Black representatives of the Indian government to poor struggling Black communities and vulnerable Black youth. The neighborhoods are infiltrated, and youths enticed-if not addicted- through the irresistible magnet of free drugs.

As stated earlier, some of these same drug induced Black youth are available to disturb violently opposition political protest and to introduce the desired racial element-and related loathing-by attacking Indian assets and Indian passersby. Of course, the Black opposition finds itself on the defensive, and blamed for racial intimidation and injury; it can neither organize effectively nor gain traction and move its program forward. This is a legacy from its own earlier sordid days, and it is constantly reminded of the fearful stench of those times. More pointedly, watching apprehensive Indians are saturated with a steady diet of what is the true color of the street, and to make no mistake as to who is responsible for their anxieties. They see black!

Some might see this as official race baiting, race mongering, or race pandering by the PPP government, while using taxpayer resources. But it cannot be denied that what this does in racially smoky Guyana is to hurl more embers in the sputtering flame. This drives more heated wedges and creates more separation between two groups already clustered in racial misgivings, suspicions, and torments. Besieged horrified Indians look on and shake their heads up and down in ready agreement and disgust. Blacks see the same things, and shake their own heads from side to side in confirmation of grounded beliefs: that Indians get away with more and more trickery, and that they use Black men and women to do their dirty work.

It never stops; there is little, if any, flexibility of thinking as to what might very well lie at the bottom of the story, such is the extent of the dark psychic conditioning on both sides.

As these litanies of perversities repeat themselves, Black resentment and Black anger solidify and rise. The distressed behold multiple injustices and indignities from using to weakening to scapegoating to dying. They simmer quietly for the most part. They are not so quiet and reserved when the violence unleashed, blood spilled, and lives destroyed are at the hands of the state, as maneuvered by lawless PPP men. And they are lawless —just look at the police force.

State Executions, Black Victims, Black Anger

It calls itself the Guyana Police Service these days; it used to be named the Guyana Police Force. The many disbelieving and critical see this as a change in name only; and 'service' does nothing to disguise a willingness to resort to lethal force without warning or due care. For most citizens, the GPS is seen as a national representation of the extent to which this society has deteriorated. It stands as an emblem of all that is wrong. Once it was the nemesis of the ruling PPP; now the GPS is its ally, and partner-in-crime. Just ask any law abiding Guyanese; but listen more closely to Black Guyanese.

Guyanese of all races look at the police and see an unending reservoir of wrongdoing, which ranges from routine corruption to chronic obstruction-and maladministration-of justice and outright felonious conduct. The races live with a body of uniformed public servants whose official existence is tied to exploitation, coercion, and general dereliction of legitimate duties. It is widely believed that a hapless society is targeted with the unspoken approval of political masters, who are trapped by criminal quid pro quos, which shackles at the institutional and political levels. These are the general across-the-board sentiments. Now try asking Black Guyanese specifically and the reaction is a storm of anger and disgust.

Black people believe with powerful conviction that they have been made special examples and prime targets, and experience the full, sometimes lethal, force of reckless extrajudicial policing. It rankles that, in most instances, the state perpetrators are Black members of the force who have come to epitomize the callous attitude, aggressive presence and heavy weight of suppression.

From the Black perspective, policemen shoot guns into houses, they shoot at moving cars, they shoot into crowds, they shoot innocent individuals, they shoot in bright daylight, they shoot under the cover of night; and when the shooting is done, guns are planted. Most of this shooting is done in the name of the state, and on behalf of the people. The bloody, deadly results, however, are overwhelmingly tilted in one direction: ONE MORE BLACK VICTIM!

Call it whatever suits the fancy, or the political correctness of the times: self-defense, corrective action, a few 'bad apples," out-of-control cops, procedural lapses, insufficient training, and so on and so forth. Regardless of the advocacy or defense proffered, this is where all roads point: There have been too many out and out executions by members of the police force and too many of the victims-if not all of them-have been BLACK. It does not mitigate in any way that the perpetrators are mainly Black. In fact, it only makes the fires of anger burn more fiercely.

Along the same lines, there is a solid, immovable, irreversible belief in Black circles-those without an axe to grind or a political agenda. It is that a good number of police killings involving Black males in the last decade involved political sponsorship or business dealings of some sort. And that introduces more racial steam and acrimony in this fractured society for this mean INDIAN fingerprints on both counts.

As if all of this is not bad enough, there is the sordid aftermath of these episodes of unwarranted, inexplicable, and unjustified violence, where the related evidentiary chain fragments into useless chaff. Repeatedly. From ballistics to bullets to bodies, everything disappears; this extends to witnesses, memories, and records. That is, if any real effort was made to gather anything of substance in the first place. There is this whole apparatus within the institutional and political spheres that is dedicated to sabotaging comprehensive, honest investigation; and to deny the administration and enforcement of law and justice. The man-in-the-street, especially the poorer one, already is familiar with such conduct and standards; he has suffered from it. From a Black outlook this means several troubling things: Black life is cheap, Black killings don't count, Black justice does not exist.

It is incredible that in this readily charged, divided local environment, such suspicious, uncalled for killings of Black men, and the ensuing cover-ups would even be contemplated, much less practiced, and then condoned. But they are contemplated and they are practiced. As a point of clarity, and an aside, there is no brief tendered here for criminals, or any denial to the right of self-defense by the police. Having said this, it is obvious that there has been, at best, chronic recklessness on the part of members of the GPF; or, at worse, wanton criminality of the most heinous sort.

In the seething, overheated cauldron of racial differences and racial enmity in this society, these killings do not go unnoticed. They are not forgotten, but chalked up as part of the increasing inventory of injury and injustice inflicted upon the local Black population by a racist party using the equivalent of Black "House Slaves." This is what pervades communities, fuels conversations, and inflames individuals, gatherings, and groups. All Black. All terribly unhappy. All incensed. Amidst the layers of discontent, reason takes flight, logic fails, and patience grows thin. Dangerously thin and daily.

How long will they be allowed to kill, to kill at random, and to kill without recourse to some iota of justice?

Occasionally the air brings mumblings of reform. The response is immediate and scathing: Such mumblings bring dismissive scorn, as talk of reform is believed to be intended to obscure what went before, and to cover more evils; that nothing of substance will change; that the key players, the dirty tricks artists (the liquidators), and the tainted seniors and juniors will all remain in place to perpetuate their lawlessness on the feeble, the undefended, and the targeted. And that means, where executions are concerned,

Black Guyanese –whether in their home, or DWB (Driving While Black), or living large and on the edge. At this time, it is almost an article of faith that the officially sanctioned irresponsibility and intermittent use of deadly force will continue in spurts against Black victims, at the behest directly, or indirectly, of Indians. That is, until there is a catastrophic breakdown and full-blown resistance to that which maims and deadens, and taunts in so many painful ways.

Remember the feeble attempts at diminution of extrajudicial activities as the work of a few "rogue cops?" The reality is that some of these characters are known serial abusers who either have dirty secrets for the regime, or have done their dirty work; they are not "few" in number. For this, they are sheltered and protected, and held in reserve to commit more serious misdeeds, when the occasion demands. Linden comes to mind, and could be a case in point, despite the haze and the self-injected amnesia. To Black chagrin and rage, matters have gotten so out-of-hand and brazen, that fingered ranks are allowed to walk through conveniently open and unmanned doors, while nearby sentinels look the other way, or absent themselves. This is the political cum security *danse macabre*, which keeps getting polished and institutionalized to the detriment of the whole country, and none more so than Black victims, Black families, and Black people.

Black Killings and the Farce of Commissions

There is more Black anger; it is centered on the Linden killings and this business of the Commission of Inquiry. The government's primary objective-maybe the only one it had in mind-was to get the protesters off the bridge and streets, and open this vital artery to the important people raising a ruckus from the hinterlands. To hell with the dead and injured. Who cares! To this end, the PPP government did what governments all over the world do when cornered: It convened a COI. To be more precise, it tricked the people of Linden (and their leaders) into believing that the truth would be bared, and justice served. Good luck, folks. Why? Because COIs are mechanisms intended to cool tempers and temperatures, provide breathing room, buy time to facilitate contingency remedial arrangements, and afford the opportunity for backdoor discussions involving adversarial parties. They can also reduce interested parties to tears, as the Linden COI results showed. On occasion, commissions deliver findings, conclusions and recommendations of substance; other times they leave a lot to be desired in the bland grayness finalized and handed over, as the Linden COI showed again. It was nugatory. When this happens, as it did here, there are now the jagged issues of review, acceptance, and implementation.

Each of these areas can be time consuming. But the government now rightly believes that it has gotten off lightly, so it is all about acceptance, closing books, and moving on quickly. Accordingly, there is no need to run the clock down, and then out through its "internal contemplations," several rounds of parliamentary back and forth, tortured behind-the-scenes negotiations, final agreement, and then partial implementation, if anything. No, it cannot believe the lack of sting in the report, or the caressing slaps on the wrist handed down to its agents and insiders for their patent and aggregated perjuries.

Clearly, the blind or the deaf could have seen that, when its senior representatives summoned before the COI pretended to know nothing and distanced themselves from any responsibility, the stage was already set. It was: GIVE NOTHING AWAY! The conclusion was foregone; the people of Linden were about to be left to drift and foam in a cloud of frustration and hopelessness. This is now the sentiment of the immediate families, an always smoldering community, and incensed supporters in other strongholds. After the hardship, sacrifice, and deaths, there is nothing to show for all that went wrong.

On the issue of monetary compensation for the victims, this much should be said: Black life is cheap; it can be bought, and it will be paid for in pittances. It is now, thanks to the COI. It should be recalled that in the aftermath of the Agricola shooting that caused the death of Shaquille Grant, the Top Cop publicly said that there were "thoughts" and the probability of compensation. This is the equivalent of do the crime, pay the fine. A prominent critic-accountant-attorney-business columnist once shared a traditional Indian saying which goes like this: "ah gun kick yuh and pay fuh yuh." This sums it all up, doesn't it? Except that now, that human life has been 'kicked' out of existence, and a national government is involved, as opposed to some rabid, out-of-control individual. Playing with lives and paying for deadly actions have now become part of the PPP's olive branch, and part of its reluctant tactic aimed at defusing Black rage.

Here are the all-inclusive questions after Linden: after all the tumult, verbal fireworks, and political sanitizing, where is the power of Black Guyanese? Where is the power to trace accountability and compel a just outcome? Where is the power to manage their destiny, even a shard of it? Where is the power of their presence? Again, it just is not there in any field.

While Collar, Brown Head, Black Shadow

Black fear and Black rage are further amplified by the double standards that apply when white collar crimes are the issue and reality. Black anguish and disgust intensifies against the *sturm and drang* backdrop of crime-fighting that claims too many Black victims-too many under suspicious circumstances-when this is placed near to rampant white collar depredations. It should be said depredations that are committed primarily by Indians, and which go mostly unpunished.

In Guyana, white collar crime covers vast lucrative areas: money laundering, procurement processes, contract awards, and the whole corruption apparatus, which is one massive ongoing national exercise in embezzlement. For the most part, connected and protected Indians bask in the glow-and glee-of golden times. These sunshine patriots plant mud and reap gems. It could be endeavors related to pharmaceuticals, construction, sale of state assets, or taxes. They put little to nothing in the system, but yet are allowed to take everything they can put their paws on, as they strip the nation's treasury to the bone. Correction —there are still more pickings lying around and waiting to be plucked. And they will be plucked by coddled, insulated, and wired Indians with the full cooperation of an Indian government.

Black Guyanese point to the unending examples of official and political protection of Indians by Indians who together collude to rip-off the state and get away with murder (literally) time and again. No Indian is charged; yet Black men are gunned down extra-judicially just for being in the wrong place, perhaps of the wrong demeanor, and definitely of the wrong color. No Indian is stripped of ill-gotten assets, but Black people are denuded of dignity, for they have little else left that can be taken away.

Through all of this, the Black man simmer, overheat, and spew in drips and spreading trickles. There is volcanic rage in some quarters, there is sharp surly resentment in others; and there is gathering discontent in every Black community and heart. The exceptions are those who are too busy helping themselves to spare a sympathetic thought for the gloom of brother and neighbor; or those Black mascots who have negotiated first-class seats for themselves at the back of the bandwagon cum gravy train.

The Black segment of the population observes all of this, and sees an interlocking complex of pyramids for which they have maps and clues. But they have neither keys nor access. Nor welcome. What it cannot see or observe, it imagines. Thus the undercurrent of Black wrath swirls tempestuously; it seeks expression and release, it is ripe for exploitation and direction. The vision in some breasts and minds, though not as yet widespread, is resigned, even apocalyptic. It is that matters must come to a head and soon; that things should be taken in one's own hands; and that let the chips fall where they have to. It is that this abomination, outrage, and racial obscenity (from either the perspective of its origins or that of its results) must be removed from the head and shoulder of the Black oppressed, and be removed by means not necessarily civil or conventional. This is what is present and grows with volcanic strength in the mind of the Black man. Let it be said here and said openly.

This is where trouble lies for this country, for communities, for its restless, anxious peoples. Unless there is revolutionary thinking on the part of Indian political leaders, meaning the ruling PPP, and on a voluntary basis, then this is the vision and horrendous reality of the future. The odds are overwhelmingly against the development of such revolutionary political thinking, and its implementation on a genuine, sustained basis. Life is too good to share; political greed and political self-centeredness inculcate blindness to the demands of the believed impotent and the increasing volatility of the frustrated and denied. *Indeed, those whom the gods wish to destroy they first make mad.*

The questions for those who lean on the fleecy crutch of doubt are these: for how long will close to two-fifths of the population submit willingly and cheerfully to a state of perpetual second place? How long will almost two out five (or three out of ten) individuals in this country live with the wretchedness of second place, as eternal underdogs, or just plain dogs? How much longer will they be content to be political nonentities, and mere shadows in the march of events? Even in the most benevolent of societies, where there is give-and-take, sharing, inclusion, understanding, and acceptance, minority groups still ardently desire and seek autonomy with their own kind.

Despite all the claims and propaganda in support of government friendship and government generosity, it has been anything but, and for all the reasons and circumstances previously identified. This is the racial poison that lurks with growing potency and speed beneath the wispy tendrils of on-and-off volcanic smoke. The concern is that a fateful eruption would occur without warning, without a known source, without specific direction, and without stated objectives. Other than to discard the hated yoke ... Such is the nature of the local racial and political contagion, where one side is usually a feared specter and the other huddled in defensive anxiety. It must be remembered that powerful natural disasters do not offer immunity. In manmade ones with a racial subtext, there are usually no innocents ...

Barren Gritty Black Communities

Black people are aware that their communities, almost without fail, have been subjected to extended and ongoing neglect. The result has been disrepair and decay, at both the infrastructural and psychological levels. On the other hand, they are just as well aware of the upgrades in facilities and amenities in which their Indian neighbors and distant counterparts have basked. There is neither attention nor money to spare for Black communities for them to grow, sometimes even to survive. Unless, of course, it is forced out of the closed mind and fisted hand of a vindictive government. That is, forced through furious protest, and only partially realized after the cacophony and blaze of confrontation, or the threatened escalation of confrontation. Even then, it is not a sustained effort to provide real relief, but temporary Band-Aids to soothe sharp tempers on the Black side, and to calm jitters on the Indian side.

For its part, the PPP government is aware that some depressed Black communities have been remorselessly squeezed into near abject poverty, and reduced to near beggary. This is not good, it should never be acceptable, and it is not a platform for peace and harmony. Not when a people brood, not when they curse the name of their oppressors (and the presence of their supporters), not when they steel themselves to sacrifice and lash out, and damn the consequences.

A strong case could be made for the Linden community in particular; there are others. It was once bustling, now it is weighed down by some seventy percent unemployment, and scant prospects, little to no government interest, and long disappeared hope. The people ask: Why do all the major works and lucrative job-enhancing capital projects have to be-must be-situated in or near predominantly Indian communities? What about the deep water harbor? What are the plans for its location? Why not in Demerara? Why can't part of the loaf be earmarked for sharing with other places where there are other faces? Meaning Black places and Black faces. Why? Why not? When, if at all? And then, how much and for how long?

These are some of the questions that sizzle and imperil with all the danger of exposed live electrical wires. Touch and there is an individual furnace; fuse a few together and there is group meltdown; gather all their naked ends in one explosive place, and there are the ingredients for racial and societal conflagration. The bodies are there in the form of the broad fragile placenta of the unemployed, the idle, the disillusioned, the disenfranchised, the locked-out, and the wrathful. This brittle cocooning racial membrane has been pushed and pulled in unbearable agony; it labors for a new freedom, no matter how stunted or premature or unrewarding. The midwife on duty is violence, fear of violence, and the disintegrating flight of peace.

In summary, the Black man in Guyana wants to chart his own course, to measure his stride and evaluate his mistakes, to manage the expectations of his journey, and to overcome the obstacles and trials in his way. He will not be satisfied, or pacified, with anything less than being responsible for carving out the extents and vistas of his horizons; and, ultimately, to live a destiny of his own choosing and under his control. Nothing else will do: not democracy, not statistical relegation; and certainly not the insult and indignity of trickledown paternalism.

This is what the PPP needs to understand, must come to grips with, and have to accept. The party's insistence on persisting with the mentality and approaches practiced so far in this country are the source of grave danger. It knows that Black Guyanese are, like American civil rights icon

Fannie Lou Hamer, sick and tired of being sick and tired. Thus, the make believe world which all inhabit threatens to shatter asunder in the slashing heat of racial rage and resentments that is known and grows. This is the abyss to which this society rushes, and yet-and yet-men who know better, who know infinitely more, refuse to recognize the flashing warning signs, which predict a coming odious reckoning, and all the devastation that such signifies. No one is listening.

CHAPTER V

Indian Dilemma, Indian Anxiety, Indian Resignation

"Life is a narrow vale between the cold and barren peaks
of two eternities. We strive in vain to look beyond the heights."
-Robert Green Ingersoll

There is a problem. To be more accurate, there are several problems for the Indian man. He is troubled, he is trapped and, to some extent, he is lost. The Indian man (and woman) knows where the problem lies, but cannot move to correct; in his mind, he dare not even contemplate, much less act. Now a clear distinction must be made right at the start: This "Indian Man" identified is one who is thoughtful, critical, and discerning; one who has a mind of his own, and a conscience, too. He sees, he hears, and he knows; he is no fool. Though he stands mentally apart from his racial brethren, he is unable-and unwilling-to go further. He will not translate thoughts, beliefs, words and disgust into tangible differentiating action. In many respects, he is a carbon copy of his brothers: anxious, but unmoving; torn, yet undecided; and resigned, though hopeful. And most of all, and just like them, he is racially loyal to a fault, to his own detriment.

Indian Dilemma

There can be no second chance. NO! A chance cannot be risked to allow the Black Man a second opportunity to grasp the reins of power. There it is in one loaded crackling nutshell. Each crackle sounds the clarion of "NO!" and "Not again!" It is a rich sweet song in the ears of his leaders; and each crackle is an expected, but fearful, spike in the side of the Black populace.

Each crackle is a loud detonation in the thunder of its unspoken finality. It cannot be uttered, for it is also the blockage in the throat, which refocuses the mind, and stalls any inclination toward experimentation, or political adventurism. There is the dark fear of the loss of a hard-earned political presence, and the equivalent of racial dilution and eventual suicide.

This is the unending fear and dilemma of the Indian voter -some of them; and which reverberate in his consciousness. For the devout there is no conflict whatsoever, since nothing could be more automatic and instinctive as voting for the PPP. It is hereditary, psychic, tribal; there is no thinking, no weighing, no deciding involved. It is what it is, what it always has been; how it will always be. But for a growing number, however, there is sturdy disenchantment first, followed by settled disillusionment, and the agitation of a powerful revulsion last. This is the totality of the dilemma of the conscientious Indian voter, which causes deep unease and unsettling concern. The same conscientious Indian voter, also thoughtful, industrious, and patriotic looks around and questions himself in this manner: How did deterioration to this appalling depth occur? Why does it have to be this way, and continue to be this way? More personally, how can I be associated with and stand for the monstrosity that is the PPP of today? Why do I have to be this way for this abomination consisting of serial crooks, pathological liars, and closet racists? How can I? How can anyone who has earned his living the hard way, cares for his loved ones, and loves this country?

Here is the conflict, the searing dilemma that propels the Indian man-mostly unwillingly-into the glare of the public square. It is a conflict engendered by the undeniably sordid, and the unrelentingly obscene. He looks around and is bludgeoned by misconduct of an egregiously disturbing nature by his elected representatives. BUT HE WILL NOT MOVE; OR BE MOVED; not for the other man! They watch and learn of chronic rapacity by the very people they vote for, rapacity taken into unchartered territory. BUT HE WILL NOT ACT; not so that a second inning could be given to the other team. There are the conflicts of overnight riches, inexplicable, untraceable wealth, and the tsunamis of dirty money and dirtier people that pollute the quality of life in village and community and town, for one and all. AND STILL ALL HE DOES IS SHRUG WEAKLY; the other folks were bad before, they promise to be worse in the future.

This is the sum of Indian fears, the dichotomies of their unending dilemmas, and the perils of a conflicted existence. This is the internal crossroad of the soul, which stares unflinchingly in the Indian face. But he himself flinches. Because at the end of the day, in the battlefield of the conscience, he shrinks away from this final probing question, which remains stubbornly unaddressed: What does this say of me as a god-fearing individual, an upright citizen, a thinking being? What does it say?

This is what is said.

Amidst the pervasive decay, the contempt, the sneer in the face, and the arrogance of the politically rewarded people, this Indian voting composite stares blankly, but resolutely, ahead in the best traditions of accessories. Because of this stance, it can be said that the thinking, concerned Indian voter is NO DIFFERENT from the diehard, fanatical, unswerving, nothing-matters-but-race traditional Indian voter; and their equivalents in the Black camp. The new, cosmopolitan, thinking Indian man is cut from the same cloth, as those who went before, and who are still very much part of the riven texture of the domestic electoral fabric.

So, the Indian man stays the course; he is afraid of what he has at present, what he helped to create; yet he is even more fearful of what change could introduce. It could be more of the current ugliness; or a repeat of the old horror. Thus, he takes no chances; change is not an option. His response is simple and final: NO to change; NO to the usurpation of Indian interests; NO to the demise of Indian ascendancy; and NO to the diminution of Indian culture. He does not want to return to yesterday. He is afraid and genuinely so. He believes that the other side, the opposition, the mainly Black opposition is waiting for its turn to steal and plunder at the public trough; and to drive Indians into oblivion with recriminatory zeal, if given a second chance. The collective tribal memory is long; it will not forget; it is unforgiving.

Then there is the plight of the poor, the unemployed, the struggling. The Indian man is familiar with the desperate straits of the poor in this country, who are daily unable to feed their families, obtain needed medicines, and live with dignity. He knows that they are many; and that they are Indian and Amerindian and Black, and mostly the latter. He empathizes with them when he can spare the thought; or remembers. He is of the view that their lot should be better, if only incrementally, given the governmental profligacy that abounds. Except that there is a lack of political concern and compassion for the downtrodden and needy, mainly Black; the political leaders are too busy taking of themselves and their own inner circle. These leaders are beyond brazen, vulgar does not begin to describe them, and iniquitous only covers part of their unsavory existence. All the while, the Indian man remains mired in a world from which he adamantly refuses to emerge or disengage.

Sure he is upset and troubled, as there is increasing evidence, and the depletion of doubt, as to the stout horror of misconduct and misrule at all levels in society. But that is all there is: he is upset and troubled. No more; just move on to the next item. But he knows in his heart that what he sees and knows and accepts, forms an intrinsic part of the observation and comprehension of his Black friend, colleague, neighbor, opponent, and fellow citizen; whether they are present in the discomfort and tension of nearness; or somewhere out there in the hazy relief of distance. Whereas the Indian man is philosophically upset, the Black man is viscerally angry. And whereas the Indian man is mentally uneasy, the Black man is emotionally burning. With this comes the jeopardy of muted anxieties, the ruffle of cultivated fears, and the paralysis of troubled history. The memories are dreadful, as they are bitter and long.

Indian Anxieties

"Twenty-eight years of darkness." What started out as a wailing threnody of oppressed anguish has been carefully nourished into a political rallying cry; it is now fully transfused into the racial mind and bloodstream. This is the throbbing, fevered reality of the Indian man —twenty-eight years of darkness; utter darkness. He cannot forget, is not allowed to forget and start afresh, but is weighed down and imprisoned by themes orchestrated and calculated to terrify and tear at his primeval insecurities. The themes are piercing and physical: looting, burning, brutality; they are draining and psychological: shortages, running, escaping. These are enough, though there is much more left unmentioned. It is also self-destructive.

First, such attitudes and postures buttress a vulgar repugnant regime that persists, that outdoes itself, in setting newer and newer levels of depravity and wanton excess. Nowadays it is widely accepted-even among Indians-that the PPP long ago surpassed the worse that was registered by the PNC in its heyday. The latter was loudly-and rightly-condemned; the PNC, however, as bad as it was (and it was) look like beginners when lined up against their successors in office. Yes, it has become this sickening and disgusting; this is how far the political vagabondage has reached.

Second, the Indian will blink, but he will not budge. He will disagree, criticize, excoriate, insult, even spit upon his racial brothers, and political benefactors; but he will not veer at the ballot box, when he turns up. This is a simple fact of Guyanese political life. So he remains stuck, in a state of deliberate helplessness and racial blandness, in a political warp and cell of his own making. Who knows, such a state might even be welcomed.

Third, there is a price for this, which is the root and branch of Indian anxieties. It is because he is seen as a subscriber to the lawlessness that passes itself for government; in no small measure, he is judged as defender and supporter and beneficiary, even when he is not. The Indian man is held responsible for making possible, through his vote and immovability, the presence of an oppressive and destructive government; one that punishes the Black man. He knows that he is seen as too condoning, and too tied to the racial umbilical cord, to the extent that he manifests neither presence nor protest nor pressure against the excesses of the PPP; and that he will not support, he will not confront, and he will not add voice to bring about change and betterment. This is the essence of his anxieties, which ricochets unendingly within his tautened nervous system.

Fourth, he is well aware that among Blacks with whom he shares space-and who might belong to the ranks of comrade, or colleague, or community, or stranger-there is terrible unhappiness and despair with the way things are, and where it leaves them. Some are openly disgusted, some are viscerally hostile, some are mutedly sullen, some are coldly distant; the patina of politeness and submissiveness has long disappeared. ALL ARE ANGRY; VERY ANGRY. More and more, conversations among individuals speak ominously of "change must come" and "there is a way to do these things." Perhaps, most ominous of all is: "there is only one way left."

In spite of the increasing evidence of all these surging emotions and attitudes, the Indian man knowingly persists, through the tormenting vale of his anxieties, with the fragile belief and scant hope that the state of things-meaning the political racial status quo and power arrangements-will continue unrevised in the same way. In perpetuity! And be allowed to continue unchallenged.

This has to be wishful thinking in the extreme, and is patently absurd. It is false and suffers from an unfathomable disregard for the aspirations of a people; an erroneous underestimation of their discontent, and, at bottom, severe dissociation from the realities that flare in the heart, and are obvious in the street of life. Think about this: During the PNC repression, fields were burned, rice planting was purposely reduced, and Indian people fled by the planeload. Further, the *Mirror* newspaper somehow stayed afloat, and served as a tiny flicker of protest —tiny, but a flickering bonding presence nonetheless though an interminable period of Indian distress and despair; other forms of protest and resistance to the oppression of the times developed muscles and gained fateful traction. The will to resist burned.

Those were the circumstances when a different group of people were effectively marginalized and subjugated. They serve as precedents, and calls for action. However, and most dangerously, there are several huge differences that stand out from those earlier days. In today's Guyana, these differences are: 1) There is the presence of a believed countless number of guns in this society; 2) there is the enormous narcotics factor and the related abundance of dirty money; 3) there is an army of available forces-some loitering unoccupied in the street, others reserved underground-that can be called upon; 4) there is another army of discontented and frustrated ex-security personnel who do not like the status quo; and 5) Black people are MORE MILITANT. Clearly, there exists the means through firepower and human and monetary resources to agitate for change by one side or to resist change by the other. Last, there is the accompanying mindset that facilitates change; and which firmly believes that change is possible and something has to give.

It is true that there is no palpable opposition; but that is chimerical, because it can reassemble itself through the merest of effort in announcing its presence and waving a flag. This is Guyana, and in less than a heartbeat, its failures and nonexistence would be forgotten. It could serve as a point of cohesion and a platform of projection in any developing turmoil. If this is not forthcoming for whatever reason, there is even greater danger. It is the danger that any local Tom (Kagame), Dick (Kabila) or Harry (Ojukwu) could step into the combustible void to galvanize the teeming, angry hordes of disenchanted and denied. Anyone would then be in a position to channel and unleash the long suppressed volcanic fury that would split the fabric of this nation into tatters of unimagined disharmony. Whatever emerges would be terrifying all around.

Call it the eternal conflict between haves and the have-nots, the favored and the disfavored; or the assembling of raw naked racial animosity; or the pursuit of justice and equity and dignity. Call it the uncontrolled madness of incensed mobs freed from their shackles. Call it whatever comforts, but this is the crux of the Indian man's great fear and steady anxieties. Amidst his recognition of chronic wrongdoing on every front-many times heavily racially smeared-there is the constant concern over sudden violent uprising and fiery upheaval. There is the dread brought about by his own reluctance, indeed resistance, to be a catalyst for expansive change. He knows that he is seen as a tacit supporter and more; an enabler that makes possible Black wretchedness. He knows that he can be an instant, accidental, or selected target. Agricola brought that home in the fires that pierced the darkness and burned the blood of attackers and victims, both distinctly racial. In those instantaneous flares-whether sponsored or instigated-it becomes clear how effortless it is for the hellhounds to be gathered then let loose. In the fleeting limiting instance of Agricola, they ran in roving isolated packs. The unstated accompanying fear is: What about when there are numerous packs and they are coordinated to complement each other for maximum effect? In other words, there is continuing distress over the threat and reality of broad-based multiple front eruptions.

Recent history has revealed to the nation that any 'Fineman' and 'Blackie', any 'Chamaar' can inflict appalling violence, wreak terrible havoc, and engender immense psychological fear for a long time. Though there was talk and suspicion of political threads, these men were first and foremost criminals, and indubitably criminally minded; but their presence was deadly, even when they were operating as Lone Rangers, or at the head of ragtag bunches. The position is this: it would be vastly more destructive to communities and nation, if group or groups, in their anger and frustrations, take it upon themselves to commit to the prime objectives of balancing the ethnic power scale, resolving the skewed ethnic equation through breaking what they consider ethnic leg irons and harnesses. AND THERE ARE THOSE WHO HARBOR SUCH ANGER, FRUSTRATIONS AND OBJECTIVES! THEY ARE MANY!

Indian anxieties are further exacerbated by the institutional exclusivism of the security forces; it is a situation to which he is a major contributor. He harbors chronic misgivings about its neutrality-and its likely dedication to constitutional responsibilities-in a real explosive state of affairs. Still, he does nothing to address or to ameliorate through his own actions. Instead, he seeks a ramshackle resolution through self-help structures (community policing) in outlying areas, and outsourcing arrangements (phantom mercenaries) when the big guns are needed. Neither brings lasting comfort.

At this juncture, there must be fleeting acknowledgment of the existence of currently dormant phantom squads. They are dormant at present in purposeful strategic retreat and obscurity, not disarmed or disbanded in disarray or through attrition. They are out there with their weapons and are no less potent today. What does this mean for the apprehensive Indian man? Has it brought him comfort or reduced the level of his fear? Does the presence of shadowy sentinels and phantom defenders resolve, to any degree, the sharp issues of right, dignity, justice, and fairness to the satisfaction of those who are nailed to the foot of the economic ladder? Is the hand of the uncaring, the underdog, the hopeless, and the determined stayed? And now for the final question: does any of this (phantoms, guns, presence and availability for usage —more on these later) guarantee peace in this mentally distraught, racially fragile and fragmented land?

The consistent answer is: No, no, and no. Because adjacent to the phantom forces, there is an army of ex-army people who have not sold their skills, expertise, and presence to the highest bidder. The latter have crossed neither political nor ethnic floor; they are too aware and concerned about the frightening lot of their own people. Thus, there were some rumblings and sparks of interest from them when their onetime Chief of Staff threw his hat in the ring. It goes without saying, that there are determined, ferociously committed men on both sides of the racial divide who can cause severe devastation to life and psyche. They have the guns, lots of guns. Everybody has guns, with the possible exception of those caught in the middle. All of this the Indian man knows to his guts. He is rightly afraid.

What about those who have nothing to lose? How about those who believe that there is much that can be gained, and with minimum investment of limb and resources? The Indian man must be cognizant of and consider what follows.

While dyed-in-the-wool party supporters might give barely passing thought to the massacres at Lindo Creek and Bartica still thickly bandaged in official cotton wool, the ordinary Indian citizen wants to know what happened at Lusignan and who is responsible. Speaking of Lusignan, Indian Guyanese know with near absolute certainty that if such a horror had been visited upon a poor, sleeping Black community, the immediate aftermath would have cataclysmic and deadly. No questions asked; let there be a real fiery, lethal rumble; no discussions, no reasoning.

Along with the truth of Lusignan, Indians have the same interest as to where the trail of the murderers of Minister Sawh ultimately leads. Even if the loyalist could care less, the thinking, honest Indian seeks clarity (and closure) on not only Lusignan and Sawh, but of all the other massacres and missing weaponry, some of which have not been publicly disclosed. And, of course, the national security operations spearheaded by a patriot resting in a U.S Federal Detention Center, and patiently counting down his days to freedom, while he plots for those who first used him, then disowned him. Again, the regular Indian citizen, as well as most Guyanese, wants to know the truth of what really went down. He wants to know.

It is of little comfort that stalwart men from top to bottom in the major political camps are compromised and that their hands are stained with blood. What matters is that both parties decided that guns and killings spoke more authoritatively-and finally-than conferences and struggles for consensus; that a fragile, hopscotch peace prevails; and that this same meager peace can be ruptured and exposed, for what it really is, in a nanosecond. Therefore, all the vacuous babble about democracy and freedoms and multicultural society and unity matter for naught, when so-called "wild men," "dangerous" men, "extremists" and unknown phantoms-political or private-are directed to take corrective action; or decide unilaterally to take things in their hands.

This is the trembling, disconcerting world of the Indian Guyanese. He works hard, he lives frugally, and he means well. But he is content to stand idly by and watch his life toil undone by bandits in suits, who also wear impressive titles, and are overloaded with loot from the public treasury. He cares, but does not care; and it is all because of the embracing hues of impenetrable tribal colors, of his unshakable racial loyalty.

So, this society hangs by the thinnest of hairs. Some-none more so than those with vested interests-will rush forward to denounce stealthily, but vehemently. They do so when faced with the everyday corruption monster. It is counterproductive and inimical to their interests and entanglements to admit to anything, even the obvious. For them, there are no racial issues of substance or merit for the most part. It would be that this amounts to baseless speculation, exaggeration and the inflammatory. They are frauds and they lie. They know so; and the really ethical and conscientious know them, too. But it does nothing for the divisive plight of the nation in general; or the consternation of the Indian populace in particular. The latter alternately hovers indecisively, lives with insecurity, and the fleeting recognition of his contributory agency. This imbues with distress, for it goes neither unnoticed nor unmentioned; and is a cause for mutual, unstated tension. Last, he knows that the so-called ABC countries are uncomfortable with the deplorable state of affairs in Guyana, but diplomatic protocol inhibits any public castigation of the PPP government. He knows that the Americans removed the PPP from power, and then reinstated it some thirty years later. And he knows that, despite the tenor of the times, the former still terrorizes his party like the sword of Damocles, by its mere presence. All of this amplifies his sense of resignation relative to dangers imagined, but lurking; calamities troubling, but only momentarily contained.

Indian Resignation

The Indian citizen has resigned himself to a number of unpalatable realities. On a regular night, he does not-cannot and will not-walk the streets of the capital city Georgetown. This is not speaking of cruising

Holmes Street or Hunter Street or America Street, to name some of the more perilous spots in the hardscrabble sections of the capital. Rather, this is about strolling down Lamaha or Robb or Church streets. He just cannot for fear of violent assault and banditry; discretion rules the feet. Then, on any unsettled day, when rumors fly and tensions suddenly escalate, the busy commercial thoroughfares empty in a long microsecond. Stores are hurriedly barricaded behind sturdy steel curtains; Indian folks race toward speedboats at the Stabroek Market, the nearby cluster of bus parks, and the relative safety of their quarters. Fear permeates the air; humiliation becomes part of the tingling, quivering skin. The powers that be responds with some garbage about "unfounded" or "malicious" and just as quickly go back to their rigid postures and thieving ways. The Indian man and woman, the fearful worker, and the cowering child are all left on their own. Their sturdy leaders, loud in the safety of guarded office and protected TV station are full of vim and pseudo machismo. And just as daringly, they slink away in haste to their mansions and castles in heavily fortified apartheid reserves away from the center of confrontation. The stranded, besieged Indian knows he has to carve out the passage of his flight by himself. He resigns himself to running a terrifying gantlet. He might have been there before. He wonders where things could lead at some point in the future, how far they would go. On this score, the Honorable Speaker of the House painted a jarring, ominous picture for all those who paid attention to his very far-reaching words.

In *Stabroek News* January 16, 2013 edition, there was an article captioned *"I should have had adequate notice of "scandalous" motion amendments –Speaker says on clerk's complaints."* In this rare public spat with the Clerk of the National Assembly, the Speaker of the House spoke of certain "scandalous" amendments made to motions before the said National Assembly. Worse yet, and more to the point, the Speaker himself is reported to have said that the amendments by PPP members contained serious allegations against named individuals, including sitting MPs from the opposition benches. These allegations were of such an explosive nature that they would have triggered "civil war" the very next day, if allowed to stand intact.

This is the Speaker in Guyana's parliament and he is quoted as using the equivalent of a national nuclear term "civil war." This is the Speaker of the House, not a foaming-at-the-mouth, wide-eyed rabble-rouser at the street corner whipping a crowd into frenzy. This is someone in the know, and who knows. Indeed, he does know what he speaks of when he mentions that telling phrase "civil war." He saw those telltale insertions on the run and by chance-it would seem-and his reaction was instantaneous and conclusive: DELETE! Delete everything! Delete now!

Pause and think about this for a moment: The Head of the Presidential Secretariat, a Cabinet ranking officer, is said to have pushed the people of Agricola to a period of uncontrolled madness. He did so through his choice-and use-of a single word: rumble. But "rumble" was only part-an infinitesimally smaller part-of a much larger story. While that word might have been the fateful, shattering straw, it means nothing when viewed in isolation. But it formed part, and was seen and heard as more, of the same infuriating injustice. Real or perceived.

Now, the Speaker is beside himself with words as written, on the sly, it would seem, for deliberation in the most august body in the land – Parliament. It prompts him to use those two words, which should not be taken lightly. They were not used irresponsibly. When taken together-the one word that reverberated on the East Bank Demerara, along with the written unknown ones from the amendments-it becomes incontrovertibly clear that this nation called Guyana is poised on an edge; one that is sharp and slippery, and extremely perilous.

It is because "civil war" identifies visceral enemies –they are there. It is that "civil war" demands partisan soldiers and boots on the ground –they are present. It can be said to be perilous, because "civil war" calls for armaments, and lots of them –they are available, too. Those who believe that this country, beneath its deceptive veneer of harmony, has solidarity and unity fool themselves, and seek to make fools of others. It is self-serving, delusional, and empty headed. Just ask the Speaker of the House. Now listen to His Excellency two months later.

The president himself used the words "hate" and "haters" several times during his address at Babu John in March 2013, while honoring party founder and hero Dr. Cheddi Jagan. He was careful enough to say that the hate was directed against the PPP. Still, no one should be fooled, and the cleverness be dispensed with immediately. If this "hate" and these "haters" focus on the PPP, then it is, by extension, directed against those who support and perpetuate the party in power. And these would be Indians.

On the other hand, the "they" referred to in his address at this sacred PPP site, before a faithful, if not fundamentalist, crowd, can only mean the PNC, which in turn means Black people. And whether said or unsaid, it reduces the concern to stark racial terms. Indeed, the bottom house incitements elevated to a public prayer at the altar in Babu John. This was not a presidential play on words, but the equivalent of shouting "fire" in a dark crowded room. This time it is true.

When "hate" and "haters" are aligned to the "civil war" fears of the Speaker, it becomes clear that the beating heart in Guyana's divided body indicates not only what the problem is not, but what it really is. It is not a social problem, a class problem, or an economic problem. It is a RACE problem. It is not about philosophical or policy differences, but mutual differences saturated with hate that is race based, and race laced. It is not an academic exercise. It is about people and power, and with both come raw, naked passions all around. Race is the cement, the acid, the poison in the national soul; it holds tenuously, but corrodes and debilitate at the same time. To date, both parties have refused to carve out an approach designed to attack this fatal societal disorder.

When anything can push this country to the brink, to the cataclysm of overnight "civil war," and when it is the contention of men in authority, men at panoramic heights, and who have holistic insights of the "hate" and "haters" massed below and around, then this land and its peoples are in dire straits; and this is a source of growing anxiety for concerned Indians. Those who wish to bury their heads in the sand and ignore reality are welcome to do so. They do so while the racial fuse burns. This can no longer be considered speculative or mischievous. Persons in their right senses, and with political antenna hallway-only halfway-attuned, would be hard pressed to deny the racial reality in Guyana. For no matter how subdued or invisible is this reality, it is very much present, and solidly so; it is poised to surge past old restraints. From any perspective, it constitutes a clear and ever-present danger to the wellbeing of ALL citizens in this country. It is the totality and state of Indian anxieties, dilemmas, fears, and resignation. Now it is time for a look at the Black Opposition.

CHAPTER VI

THE PNC ~VITAL NATIONAL PRESENCE OF FADED RELIC

"The credit belongs to the man ... whose face is marred by sweat and dust and blood; who strives valiantly; who errs and comes up short again and again; ... and who if he fails, at least fails while daring greatly ...."
-Theodore Roosevelt

Amidst the countless demoralizations of daily existence in Guyana, there is an urgent-no, desperate-need for a counterforce. A counterforce that is viable, visible, vigorous. It must represent an option, offer solace, embody hope, and give strength. Such a counterforce must be a presence: formidable in stature, perspicacious in outlook, and focused on change. To do these things, to be this way, to live for these purposes, it must be about care, public service, and identification with the sufferings of the peoples, and possessing of a fierce, unrelenting determination to lift them up; to make one and all, and a nation, better. There is one major problem with all of this: it is NOT happening here.

Vital National Presence or Faded Relic

The PNC does not know what to do without power; it does not know what to do with itself. This is a national tragedy in and of itself. Supporters, foes, and observers have watched as the party has grown fat, lazy, complacent; even stupid at times. Other than for the diehards, a surprising number will agree that it is inconsequential in the face of racial imperialism. The party lolls comfortably-too comfortably-in the doldrums of a self-inflicted apathy, an untreated malaise. It does so to the chagrin of its own people first, and then to the disbelief of concerned onlookers.

From all appearances, the PNC is lost; the bigger deficiency is that it has no interest in finding itself, in committing to the hard task of revitalizing and reinventing itself. Its presence and condition is characterized by a lack of energy, lack of strategy and accompanying tactics, and lack of a permeating vision. All of this is highly visible, and screams from the rooftops. When it should be strong, it is a shadow; when it should be a force, it is a whimper; and when it should be recognized and respected, it is dismissed. This has engulfed its core base of supporters. Meaning that disillusionment has taken a powerful hold on Black Guyanese. Now they wonder if there is a way out of the present bondage for them, if there is a way forward.

First, there is the leadership legacy: It is widely believed, even in the upper echelons of the party-that there has been tawdry compromise, outright sellout, and sustained failure at key times and in crucial areas; that the concerns and priorities of Black Guyanese were sacrificed in the temple of self-interest and self-promotion. The fallout continues in the form of anger, disgust, and resignation. There is pain and hostility, too. Pain at the feeling of being betrayed; and hostility at those believed responsible, be they part of the party's house; or from the suffocating political shroud on the outside. The stricken wonder if the only solution left is to take matters in their own hands and damn the consequences.

Second, there is the assessment-perhaps, inaccurately-that current leadership is too focused on structure and methodology, on the finer points of engagement, and on the orthodox. None can disagree that the PNC has been outhustled and outmaneuvered by the PPP in most instances, and in some cases clearly outthought. There is the perception that it is preoccupied in managing the newest manufactured crisis, while the streets and communities are left unattended and largely to their own devices. There is hidden danger in leaving the anger and aspirations of a people dangling: it spawns the unthinkable; it gives life to the impressionable, the reckless and the uncaring; it raises the specter of headless, uncontrolled splinter groups. To sum this up, the PNC is nowadays seen as too slow on the draw, too distant from the pain, too unconcerned with daily realities, too uninspiring in its presence and, like the PPP, too much about itself. It keeps losing ground and particularly on the race question, which festers and drips and smells.

Whereas the PPP has made racial manipulation a substantial, and sometimes, stealthy plank in its approach and practice, the PNC has been content to let race matters linger as they have always been, and as they have been always perceived. The result is wariness and worry on the part of Indians, and mismanaged, unfulfilled expectations on the part of Blacks. For both races, this is the equivalent of an exposed nerve in the midst: it is live and raw; it throbs and agonizes. The body is stricken and doubled over; it is also on edge. Much of this accrues to the disadvantage of the PNC. But it adamantly resists changing its settled mannerisms and ways. The party needs to reinvent itself quickly. And drastically.

Reinvention: First -The Obstacles and Image Problems

For starters, the PNC has two major problems, both of which are image related, and both of which undermine its feeble, haphazard efforts at rehabilitation. In the first instance, there is the albatross of its ignominious past, which it is not made to forget; and which Indian Guyanese are always encouraged to remember. In the second instance, it suffers from an enduring similarity to the PPP; it is almost a mirror image of the other. Both have a history of cheating and thievery on a massive scale: one at the polls and the other at the public trough. Both have a history of appalling violence –be it polls related or street delivered; be it in militant, mobilized communities through political henchmen, the use of criminals, or the employment of mercenaries. In terms of violence wreaked on society, both are one and the same leopard –the spots are indistinguishable. The legacy is that the two competing races remember; and when they don't, they are forbidden to move towards the vital pathways of understanding, forgiveness, and a fresh start. No way! Not today! Not here!

Further, the PNC has lost its command of the street; perhaps of the hearts and minds of its own, too. Recent mobilizations have pointed to a dissipation of strength, to the absence of a sustained presence, to a lack of interest and cohesion and purpose and spirit. Now this pushes to the heart of the matter. Remember that this book is about race, racial politics, racial division, and racial discontent. With this as context, the street was seen as the easy way out. It offered intimidation, assault, and viciousness with a heavy racial flavor. Commuters, women, the elderly, and property all came under attack. Indians reeled; they emptied the streets; they retreated with their scars, and with their humiliations and indignities. And they remember. Remember frequently. Remember in graphic fearful terms, as shared by victims, and blown up in the endless retelling by those never close to the scenes of mayhem.

Today, the PNC first seeks to extricate, then distance itself, from this self-created morass, but finds a disbelieving audience. The patience, the discipline, the new tactics, new strategies, the sustained efforts, and bodies so obviously needed are in short supply. The party's supporters are barely listening, they refuse to nibble. Enthusiasm for the long, tedious, demanding, backbreaking, unrewarding work is palpably scanty, and proving to be a hard sell; if it is sold at all. For too long, the mental conditioning, the emotional response, and the physical reflex had been to attack and dismantle. Not anymore. In today's world, the mayhem of the streets has severe handicaps; it is counterproductive, and self-defeating.

What is the alternative? What has not been tried? What is left to try? This has been said before, it must be said again now: Regardless which party is in power, this society needs a strong, meaningful opposition, if only to keep government honest, as part of a respected system of checks and balances, and for the sake of national sanity.

Reinvention -The Hand Outstretched

The PNC, like its nemesis the PPP, is immovably set in its ways. It knows what is wrong, and where it misses the boat. The party, however, refuses to heed good sense, and commit itself to the long, new struggle to overcome its past, to shed its baggage. It has not demonstrated either the willingness or interest to implement two very vital strategies; to live them. The first is to embark on a campaign of <u>sustained outreach</u> to the Indian community. Here the PNC has been reluctant to attempt a comprehensive, continuing outreach of a genuine nature. Sure, it has engaged in the occasional stiff, unpersuasive 'walk around' and then there is only the broad canvas of blankness afterwards. Nothing more, except for telltale absence and silence.

The party satisfies itself, like the PPP, by going through the motions on national holidays to extend the usual word about the need for unity and brotherhood and light across the racial chasm. These greetings are so useless, that they are laughable. They are exercises for the record and doomed to futility. They are just one more forgettable moment in a poorly played game.

Look, it can be argued-and has been-that the races are so inseparable from known political identification, so set in their stances, that all the outreach in the world would not make a difference when it counts. That is, at the polls. And that none is more committed to historical voting patterns, none more immovable than the Indian Guyanese. So there! In the same instance, it could also be posited; perhaps more accurately, that real outreach has never been tried, and put to the test. Real outreach that incorporates determined and focused groundbreaking, frank discussions, hard give-and-take, and the beginnings of understanding. The beginnings of understanding-hesitant, limited, searching, hopeful-would represent the flimsiest of starts, and should not be mistaken for understanding itself, or representative of any semblance of acceptance. But here is the key: it is a start, and one that is intended to be built upon.

What could be gained, if anything?

At the very least, there would be the manifestation of a real presence, a sustained one; the indication of interest that recognizes and tables the delicate issue of dealing with Indian concerns and Indian anxieties; and the extension of reciprocal good faith, if not the birth of inklings of trust. Make no mistake: this is an arduous undertaking, but doable. It is worth the try. The stark reality is neither party has gone anywhere near to such contemplations, much less action. The fallout has been racial standoff, racial suspicion, and racial fear all around.

But that is not all, for it goes without saying that the PPP is not going to stand still, and encourage garlands of welcome to the political enemy. It is sure to go into overdrive to sabotage and diminish any such efforts. The racial status quo is fine; and the PNC by its own action and inaction has contributed heavily to this situation. Additionally, each party has to be conscious of its core supporters-the diehards, the fanatics, the racists-and the sure-to-follow disagreement and resistance with too much time and attention being extended to members and communities of the other camp. Such is the mentality that has taken hold here.

Also, there is sure to be skepticism from Indians, as they are aware that the late Winston Murray ran into a steel wall when he stood for leadership of the PNC. Among the internal reactions from the powerful stalwarts at that illuminating Congress was: "A ------ man for head of this party? No way. No time." And there was this gem, so lustrously expressed by a PNC trench warrior, now parliamentarian, "Ah luv Winston like a brother, but de hair, de hair ...." And more conclusively, "Burnham nah bill dis party an lef am fuh a _____ man come and run am."

Indians are familiar with some of this, just as Black people know of the parallel Luncheon gambit, which ended in the same desultory result. Innovative thinking of such radical nature is frowned upon, and strangled out of existence. It provides sharp illumination as to what powers the engine and spins the wheels in the Congresses of local Klansmen and women; the white sheet and burning crosses are missing, but the racial slip shows.

Clearly, race is the defining and final factor, if not the only one. And just as clearly, if men who have dedicated their whole lives to serving their respective political groups cannot be trusted, will not be supported, and must not be empowered to take the helm and lead from the front, then what is there left to say? What trust and concern can there be for the wider racial segments, not one's own? Can anything constructive be said as to the authenticity and solidity of race solutions (nonexistent, to be sure) in this country, as represented and projected by either party?

What could be said is that the possible vistas that might have beckoned and been scaled are lost, and so too the opportunities that came with them. Gone are the opportunities to set precedent, to inculcate confidence, to endeavor to bridge the chasm, and to give this society a chance. It has not occurred with the PPP. It is not happening with the PNC. It has not been experienced before, and it is not going to be lived anytime soon in Guyana, perhaps never. And this promises terrible peril for the races and society.

An outreach strategy should have been the first turbine in the self-reinvention engine of the stalled and short-circuited PNC. It has been found to have no merit, has gained no traction; maybe not even the consideration within the inner sanctums of the party. Still, all is not lost, as there is one more option available: It is one from which most flinch: It is the long, difficult road of sacrifice.

Reinvention: The Challenge of Sacrifice

Sacrifice, particularly political sacrifice, is demanding, punishing, and unsatisfying in Guyana. It is why leaders and parties resort to the easy, convenient ace of race. Why travel another route to reinvent the wheel, when this surefire, guaranteed winner is available for the taking; and when it is available and submissive to manipulation. Like the PPP, the PNC has grown comfortable and complacent with the race card; it will not budge; it refuses to move out from under the comfort zone of its palm tree. Instead, it embraces and pursues the racial quick fix.

Thus, the called for sacrifice of patient, uphill struggle, and of painful, plodding progress measured in inches is avoided or dismissed outright. The knee-bending, back-breaking, resolve sapping tasks of appealing, organizing, cajoling, persuading, energizing, and inspiring to its own faithful first-and across the divide thereafter-are nonexistent in form and substance. The spirit is just not there, and the same can be said for the tactics and strategies.

There is no instant gratification, to be sure, in the Spartan approach: no praise, no glory. Indeed, there might be little receptivity and less enthusiasm for sacrifice, given traditional expectations of fixing the ballot and suppressing ensuing resistance. Because these inclinations and expectations of the party's core no longer hold; distracted, disenchanted supporters must be sold on the strategy of convincing, rather that of coercing; of overwhelming the mind, instead of overpowering the body.

History has furnished inspiring precedents and bright guiding lights. These precedents demonstrate that the oppressed people of one race will protest; that conscientious members of another will support them financially, spiritually, and physically; that intransigent, race-touting, fear-mongering politicians will tremble and think and blink. And change would follow. Change will come, but it would not be easy. Remember: sacrifice.

There are the glittering, awe-inspiring precedents of Selma and Greenwood and Montgomery. There is the history of Alabama, Mississippi, and South Carolina. There was the core, the crowd, and the different colors, too. There were the simple, poor, uneducated people with cause on their lips, resistance in their hearts, and the future on their weary marching feet. Their cause was simple: End injustice, end oppression, end inequality. End the oppression of injustice in all its forms, and none more so than the racial. What is the cry in Guyana today, if not the same? Where is the PNC when it is needed? Where are those leaders in the opposition who are not so busy taking care of self (through their own individual power sharing and rewarding arrangements) that they care to struggle and sacrifice for change and betterment of the many? Do they care as to how they are seen? Do they care enough to see what went before?

There was the vast reach and anchor of the church; there were the servants, cooks, nannies, porters, and farmers; and there were genuine, caring leaders too who identified deeply with the pain and despair of their less fortunate brothers. Again, the question must be asked: where are these same things in Guyana? Where are these motivators and inspirations?

Revisit the start of this chapter, and that damning evaluation of 'fat, lazy, and complacent.' It stands. It stands as an enormous tribute to callous indifference, and comfortable retreat. Clearly, there is an urgent need for reinvention, to start anew. And it starts with the recognition of what succeeded elsewhere, where the odds were mountainous, and what is so desperately need here. It begins with sacrifice, it is buttressed by outreach.

While all this remaking and recalibrating is contemplated, let this unassailable truth be remembered and recognized: It was not the menacing men in their berets, bullet studded bandoliers, and combat boots who brought about-who forced-change. No! It was the seamstress, the student, and the sharecropper. They all had very little to give, except of themselves. They willingly gave of that, they laid all on the line: the risk of job loss; the lack of physical safety emanating from state and communal violence; the assaults on personal dignity through spit and stick and rocks; the disappearance of the chance for higher education (a family first); and the lusterless gleam of the future. All of this failed to intimidate or to deter. This was about what is right, what is just. It was John D. Rockefeller, Jr. who said *"I believe that truth and justice are fundamental to an enduring social order."*

Thus, even as racial humiliation was challenged and grappled with at close quarters, and the tyranny of race resisted, there was still room for inclusivity, as tactic and strategy; and as part of a broad grand vision of the brotherhood of man. But the terrible, bitter sacrifices had to be made, to be lived. There was no other way left.

So the dogs, the nightsticks, the water hoses, the guns, and the rest of the apparatus of State objection and suppression were all faced down and overcome. Jail, no bail! The thinking and strategy implemented was to freeze the streets, filibuster the courts, and overcrowd the jails; and with more reserves waiting in the wings to fill the void left by those willingly carted away. No resistance, no violence, no retaliation. Organize. Persuade. Inspire. There was no need for the race card. There was no place for intimidation, assault, looting, or for opportunistic criminality. There was none of this in the face of intense, unrelenting provocation at the hands of a hostile, aggressive community and State. There was just too much discipline.

This is sacrifice. This is what compelled Orville Faubus to retreat; what forced Wallace to the defensive; and what moved the hedging Kennedys to take something of a stand. The result speaks across the decades to Guyanese today: waters parted, the tide turned, a people uplifted, and history created. Stirring, nonviolent history on the sore backs, aching feet and battered bodies of the disciplined, the committed, the believing. It still moves today. This knowledge is here in plain sight in Guyana for those who dare to use it, to sacrifice for betterment. Thus it must be asked: What place is there for the scythe of racial violence and turmoil as the answer to oppression and deadlock? Who would want to make such their trump card, when a nobler, more rewarding-but incrementally harder-way exists? When in the words of Rev King, there can be "subpoena of the conscience of the nation ..."

The ruling PPP and the opposition PNC are both fully aware of what sacrifice can do, where it can lead, and the much needed changes it can force upon this society in terms of equity and what is fair. The rulers shrink in fear from just such a development based on the sheer grit of sacrifice that is nonviolent and sustained; they will disrupt through their own wicked, clandestine infiltration to add racial undertones to any such effort through scare tactics, and the application of contagious violence. The PPP has grown efficient at manufacturing and maximizing visible racial "collateral damage." It cannot-and will not-allow such a development to take hold.

For its part, the PNC has shown itself lacking the steeled stomach to venture into hostile racial territory with palm upturned and hand outstretched. It has neither patience nor belief nor dedication to such daunting racial overtures. To the delight of its political foe, it persists in remaining behind the barrier of racial homogeneity, and reinforcing the racial silo housed within, despite the attendant weaknesses of numbers, malaise, resources, and limited vision. Both barrier and silo contain ancient wildfires that are smoking in spots, and burning in wide swaths. Like a capped volcano, the combustible energy within the tight silo seeks an opening to vent and to spread in the throes of convulsion. It rumbles ominously.

To date, the opposition PNC has sent clear and convincing signals that it lacks the interest-indeed, the guts-to roll-up sleeves and buckle down to marshaling the logistics geared towards a strategy of sacrifice-sustained sacrifice-which opens first the eyes of this nation, then its heart, and last its collective soul. It is unable and unwilling to start with its own people first, and then say to the rest of the Guyanese world: This is who and how we are. This is what we are about. This is how and where we want to belong. Rightfully so. This is sacrifice and agitation dedicated to the erosion of injustice and the attrition of oppression. It is for us and for others in this land, too.

Can this be done? Is it achievable in the jagged, treacherous, bitter context of Guyana? The answer is profound, as it is simple: YES!!! Only that this grueling road to freedom has never been embarked upon. Now in the absence of sacrifice, and the resistance to a new approach, this is what lurks, this is what threatens, this is what imperils. There is only the volcano ... Or resignation to an eternity in the discontent of the gutters, on the periphery, and in the middle of a roiling endless nowhere. The questions that resonate are these: Can the PNC ever rediscover-reinvent-itself? Or is this society to remain afflicted with the malevolence of the one party cancer? And is it ultimately doomed to the inevitability of savage unprecedented conflict?

Reinvention: Limitations and Obstacles

The PNC is burdened by many weaknesses –some are self-inflicted, some are circumstantial.

First, it suffers from a lack of funding, and other vital resources. This has severely restricted its efforts-perhaps, thinking-to mobilize, to build critical mass inside and outside the party.

Second, the party and its leadership reel from a catastrophic failure of energy, strategy, and delivery. It is seen to be unfocused and distracted, and surprisingly lacking in perspicacity. All of this has inhibited the development and tabling of any new vision either for its core supporters, or the country as a whole.

Third, time and again, the party has been found to involve itself in superficial, sketchy, unpersuasive race engagements; it recoils from the meaningful; it retreats from the untried. It has been its own worst enemy, and its adversary is only too willing to help it along in the commission of political and racial hara-kiri.

Fourth, while it is true that both political hegemons have been guilty of identical repugnant conduct in the racial swamps, the PNC has been injured the most, has fallen the farthest. And yet, it is content with itself, its standing, and its results.

Last, the PPP has the resources, the machinery, the bodies, and the unquenched desire to drive home its points and sow racial mischief to the unending disadvantage of the PNC and its bloc of Black supporters.

The ruling party has seized every opportunity to remind its loyal and wavering through reviving ugly racial memories, frequent thrusting of the old stained racial knife, and reopening poorly healed wounds around its campfires, under the bottom-houses, and in its shrines. The reminders are always the same: The PNC was the first to cheat. Like most marriages, it is now to be distrusted permanently, and never forgiven; it has lost its moral place, and cannot be considered a trusted equal partner anymore.

On its own behalf, the PNC has played along through a hard refusal to baring its past and putting things on the table. It has not demonstrated any inclination to clearing the air, or pursuing a different course. Given its own intransigence to racial outreach and inclusivity, the PNC's attitudes serve as icing on the PPP's cake; the latter has run amok knowing full well that it has a wounded floundering enemy in the first instance, and a virtually captive constituency in the next. As a group, the PNC thinks of itself first, its people second (or fourth or fifth), and country somewhere down the line. These are the circumstances and the obstacles lived by the party; it is fertile ground for the atrocities and injustices to keep multiplying.

Reinvention —Possibility or Losing Proposition

The Opposition PNC has shown itself to be a faded and fading penumbra, plagued by lack of internal cohesiveness, and smarting from the presence of growing outward disinterest. Recent practices have caused wonder in some circles as to whether it is still compromised; the shadow minister for finance was prompted to complain publicly of being "undermined" by his own. Recent circumstances have indicated that it is unable to plan and execute any strategy that compels tangible, meaningful, durable change.

If it cannot do so among its own people and in its own strongholds-targeted, besieged, and depressed-how can it rise to the challenge of doing so for outsiders similarly distressed and demoralized? When the times demand thoughtful concentrated action, it cannot motivate the people; it disappears into silence and innocuousness. It keeps its clothes clean, shoes shined, nails manicured, and hair perfectly coiffed.

Nothing seems to galvanize the party into outrage, into movement, into resistance. Remember sacrifice? Not police killings. Not uncontrolled governmental knavery and piracy. Not constitutional violations. Not daily societal assaults and other chronic obscenities. No, nothing can drive it into lifting itself from what has become a self-defeating frame of mind. Nothing!

During all of this, the PPP rocks with glee; it grows stronger, more reckless. It ventures into more and more suspect activities; its conduct is more scornful and dismissive. Many observing citizens curse, rage, and wish for all manner of dark developments to halt the political sickness, and to reverse the contamination of the racial and social sewage. There is tremendous danger in such dark ruminations and darker calculations. It is that in the absence of a credible recognized opposition-one that is in the vanguard of confronting government and circumstances-then an inviting vacuum is created. At any time, such a vacuum can be invaded by the mindless mob; multiple, organized or disorganized mobs of unknown origins, unknown leadership, and unknown objectives. But there would be known peril and known devastation. Undoubtedly, such mobs would come into being with particular racial ingredients, and singular racial intents.

The odds are not in favor of an intervening, representing, arbitrating opposition; that looks more like a losing proposition than a solid likelihood. Given the existence of a compromised security apparatus, a corrupt ruling party, vested narcotics interests, and dormant phantom forces (sometimes all part of the same indistinguishable mix) the innocent citizens of this country are all vulnerable and unprotected —be they brown, black, or indigenous. And there is the weaponry at hand to make all possible fears realized. The people are on their own, and they thrive on demonizing the disliked other. It is almost instinctive.

CHAPTER VII

RECIPROCAL RACIAL MISPERCEPTIONS, MISTRUSTS AND MISDEEDS

"Death plucks my ear and says, Live –I am coming."
-Virgil

What do most Indians and Blacks think-really think-of each other? How do each look at the other? What are some of the misperceptions harbored and nurtured? How do these same misperceptions-some public, some well-grounded, many without foundation or merit-impact the state of relations between the two fiercely competing races in their closed limited space? Why are there the generalizations and stereotypes? Why the deep and abiding mistrust? What about what is shared, what is common to both, is there any recognition of this? In the first place, are there ever such binding things as unifying values and ideals, of a harmonious national vision?

Indian and Black Perspectives: Physical and Financial

There is deeply rooted in the psyche of the ordinary Indian and Black citizenry certain unmoving beliefs. They divide, they harm. These citizens include villagers, the man-in-the street, the devout, and the laborer who eke out a living by the sweat of the brow in fields or on the road, and who are engaged in blue collar, lunch pail occupations. On occasion, they have vented and shared what lies concealed in the recesses of the mind. It can be ugly. These same disturbing beliefs are most likely present in the hearts of some of the more educated, sophisticated white collar crowd: the managers, the professionals, the technical experts, those who know better; or ought to know better.

It should be said that this group of regular citizens deliberately excludes the hardcore racists from either side; those who have proudly attested to the condition of wanting to puke at the sight or presence of the other. No, this is not about the "raw wrenk" foaming-at-the-mouth extremists. It is about the thoughts and feelings of the men and women from both racial sanctuaries, who might object strenuously to the label of "racist." They are not a minority. Some readers should brace themselves; perhaps, they might even see themselves described and highlighted. As a warning, it is not pleasant, but searing, even offensive. Then again, the truth about self, and of how things really are, usually hurts; is rarely palatable, and almost never admitted.

There are some Indians-many Indians- who see the Black man as lazy, unproductive, hostile, aggressive, predatory, criminally inclined, focused on conspicuous consumption, instant gratification, and government subsidy. Further, the Black man is believed to be lacking in the harsh Calvinistic tendencies of frugality, saving, and sacrifices. In sum, he is bereft, for the most part, of the discipline for self-sufficiency and seeks the easy way out at the expense of others. In Guyana that would most likely mean Indians. Finally, the racist inclinations of the Indian man are not of the in-your-face variety; it is more subtle: Never will he slip and publicly utter a slur, an "N" word, or scorching criticism. His cultivation is below the surface – slick, smooth, almost unobtrusive. But it is there!

In their turn, some Black Guyanese-many of them, see the Indian man as passive, covetous, corrupt, tricky, manipulative, and lacking in intestinal fortitude. He believes that the Indian will scheme and kill for "house and land;" that he will not stand up for what is right; and that he puts down the Black man, by relegating him to the ghetto of outcasts and undesirables. And the Black man has less of an issue with publicly venting hurtful slurs, or adopting aggressively intimidating stances.

80

In a nutshell, this is the depth and extent of staunch mutual misunderstanding, misreading, and error propagation. A careful look reveals that both sides hold powerful, deep seated beliefs that the other is Machiavellian, even diabolical. This is the virulent strain that courses beneath the thin civility, beneath the dull surface sheen. These substantial feelings and beliefs are not diminishing, but intensifying given the political climate, and the decreasing opportunity and increasing equity gaps. In the midst of both tribes, these hard sharp feelings find welcome and a home. These are the ugly conversations and jagged feelings shared amidst the confining comfort of one's own —be they close family, trusted friends, durable neighbors, and likeminded colleagues. The cauldron stirs, it develops texture and flavor; it is the refuge of the denied, the victimized, the trapped, the frustrated, and the overwhelmed. The contributory ingredients reinforce tribal bones and sinews erected on misgivings, disappointments, and fears.

What do the realities of everyday interactions-the presumption and actuality of physical proximity-provide in support of these contentious statements and positions? What do the internalized calculations, the stereotypical judgments, and the reflexive conjectures-be they expressed or otherwise-tell? What do they reveal as to self and each other? Where do they lead? Economics and money is as good a place to start as any. Try these beauties.

An unknown, independent Indian man passing by in a car is automatically a "government man," a "PPP hack," or a beneficiary of corrupt activity. He must have stolen millions, lives high on the hog, and is a standing member of the local 700 Club. That would be 700 million dollars minimum. It does not matter that there might be no affiliation whatsoever to the PPP; that there is tremendous contempt for the vulgarity of the ruling party. The sturdy conviction of the Black street and the heart is "dah is another teef maan." And "de guvment gat dem real good; deh livin high, high." All slurs and expletives are omitted.

Similarly, just as unfavorably and quite routinely, the Black professional-the clean, ethical Black professional-inspires demeaning typecasting, as he cruises by on his set of wheels. The measurement is that he has to be a drugs man. This evaluation is heightened if the driver is younger, sleek, coldly menacing, and rapping loudly. He is a walking, driving, jiving one-man criminal cartel, who did not earn his money the hard way, and can be up to no good.

Notwithstanding the understanding that some stereotypes might contain heavy kernels of accuracy, and that Guyana is both drug haven and easy money place, this is the gut reaction by a great many individuals from within the racial outposts, be they rural or urban. It is firm; it gathers momentum when shared with a closed homogenous crowd; and it soars into full flight when the latest sensational report of blood, death, and corruption dominates conversation and day. Point proven, belief reinforced, case closed.

Violence Ancient and Current: Complicity and Responsibility

For now, the focus remains on economics and money just a little longer, but with incremental political fingerprints and the tincture of violence. Indians remember, and live with the horror of choke-and-rob and kick-down-the-door banditry. They believed before, and continue to believe now, that this was government instigated, and government powered. That is, a Black PNC government. The physical and psychic scars remain, and they are rubbed raw easily. Indian political operators are only too willing to provide assistance with sandpaper, required rubbing, and pungent antiseptic reminders.

In a similar vein, Black Guyanese look at drug activities, drug influence and power, and drug killings; the unhesitating stance is that this area is populated mainly by Indians who use Black gunmen to kill Black men. Thus, there is anguish and injury, which can be sourced to the enemy enclave, which enjoys the full backing of the government of the day. This time, it is an Indian government. So from a Black perspective, the awful convergence of illegal drugs, dirty money, violence, murders, race, and politics points incontestably in one direction, and one direction only: the other side, the Indian enemy camp.

Observations from the ground and plain old fashioned commonsense lend credence to the postures and conclusions of both Indians and Black Guyanese, who have been victimized by individual battery, community mayhem, or racial desecration; or all three in tandem by their governments through complicity and indirect responsibility. This is the sanguinary history and stabbing present that confront this nation in the face, and which no one in power dares to admit; or ventures to address, whether they are aging grievances or fresh depredations. In the sacred spaces of both racial worlds, strong emotions are grounded in the belief that the government of the day, of the other man has subjugated them using a variety of contrivances and intermediaries.

While this has been a boon to the political actuaries and schemers, the little Guyanese man, regardless of color, has been squeezed pitilessly and left with only the solace of bitterness and unfulfilled needs, as he licks his mephitic wounds. It is a small matter for him to find convenient racial scapegoats across the boiling racial chasm, and to hold his fellow sufferer, even if innocent, accountable for his woes and harsh realities. The questions raised are: How can this society find a way to be different, to help itself to start with a fresh, clean slate? Is this possible? How? And who takes the first steps? But that is another story. There are other (mis)perceptions other ones to tell right now. It is time to trace that poison in the national bloodstream —corruption.

White Collar Assaults and Felonies

Indians complain bitterly that institution after institution is arrayed against them; that they are disrespected and denied fairness; that they are discriminated against and have to pay for everything ranging from basic documents to complex undertakings; and that they are coerced and preyed upon daily by people in uniform and people behind the counter, whether apprentice or veteran. It should be stated that the representatives of these public institutions are, for the most part, Black; and there is the belief that they have grown rich on the backs of Indians.

For their part, Black Guyanese are loud in sharing their own unhappy experiences, where they are denied place and equivalence. They look at the distribution of the state's business, and observe the unprecedented arrangements made under the table, through back channels, and secretly, towards the favored. There is the flood of largesse in the unknown millions that goes to family and friends, and where Black Guyanese do not have a ghost of a fair chance. Black people indignantly point to these obscenities and ask:

How can Indians even begin to speak of corruption? How do they dare to speak of petty corruption, when grand theft on a gargantuan scale is the order of the day for the ruling regime and its thieving henchmen? Further, where is the uproar when hundreds of millions of scarce taxpayers' resources (including Black taxpayers) are misspent, siphoned off, and trucked away by primarily Indian overseers and Indian beneficiaries, who then flaunt their tawdry opulence in the face of one and all? Where is the disgust when the occasional culprit who is accidentally exposed is subjected to the breast feeding of mock transfers and farcical resignations? How about this? Why the silence now and inaction? There are no answers, only deepening sullenness.

And as the simmering resentments build in Indian and Black minds, both look back, then build steam to embrace that first true founding father of the nation –political corruption, party corruption.

The First True Founding Father

The saga of Guyanese political corruption courses through the veins; it chokes hand and voice and mind. It is birth certificate; it is passport; and it is the national racial identification card.

Indians retain bitter memories of being cheated by election rigging and Black political treachery. There are unforgettable memories whose origins can be traced to fifty years ago and counting; alongside are-the sometimes no longer walking, but still breathing, living-monuments to keep the fires of another time warm. These memories sour conversations, color most thinking, sully nearly all relationships. This is the nature of this particular pit bull that will not release it viselike hold, will not let go. It inflames, it tears apart.

In the same way, Black Guyanese feel that Indians are no less guilty or treacherous, in that having publicly committed presence and support for their party over the years turned around and betrayed that same party beginning with the national polls of 1992. And the betrayal came in the name of racial allegiance. It does not matter to Black people that such public association and support from Indians came about through force of circumstances, and was patently superficial and artificial, if not farcical. What matters is that each race, in its own way, maintains a stranglehold on bitterness and hard, terminal feelings: the other group cannot be trusted, it is cheating and wicked. Thus, the feelings intensify irreversibly, irremediably.

Moving from what is the embedded corruption in the trenches of daily life, and past the political corruption at the national level, it is now opportune to peer into the social and civic sphere, first at street level, then at the individual and family level.

A Roiling Milieu of Suspicion and Vindictiveness

Start at the marketplace. For the most part, both races gravitate consciously, or unthinkingly, towards sellers of their own kind. Black people operate under a handicap, since most of the vendors are Indians. To be sure, there are the regular customers of both stripes, who "crossover" and spend their money. But there are many who entertain the lurking suspicion that there are "different prices for different folks." Or the stallholder tried to "pull a fast one" and that "cheating and tricks" are always part of the consideration. And that race features prominently in these sleights-of-hand. It does not matter that all shoppers might have been subjected to the same sharp practices. Race is all that is seen, and it does sometime erupt in the shrillest of ways. For their part, Indians are distraught with Black people who have problems paying the going price, who are sullen, and sometimes hostile. Or worse yet, those brazen Black shoppers who hover for the opportunity to lift merchandise. In contrast, Blacks believe that Indians withhold product, services, and courtesy, to the disadvantage of the Black buyer, when items are in short supply. Indians have expressed similar concerns when they venture occasionally to shop at Black owned stalls and stores. The inevitable, comforting, reaction is to stick to one's own, and only cross the racial barricade on a "can't help" basis. Now it is forward to the wider street, the violent street.

During violent out-of-control street protests in Georgetown, numerous Indians have been targeted and brutalized. At these times, office bound Black Guyanese-educated, socially conscious, probably churchgoing-looked from their perches, or through their windows, at the racial mayhem in the streets and had a good laugh. The concealed refrain from near and far was: "dah gun teach dem a lesson." Along the same lines, when Black victims-including the innocent and unwary-are gunned down in the street, be it officially or privately, there is quiet relief and rejoicing in Indian hearts. The prevailing sentiment is: "shoot dem, get rid ah dem." This is the nature and breadth of local racial idealism and dedication to the fundamentals of civility and what is right.

So much for the distemper of the streets. What happens at the individual and family level? In the sanctuaries of home and marriage and church?

The Verbal, Mental, Moral, and Spiritual -Disgrace and Disgust

No one can say for sure, or will trumpet any of this from the rooftops; but are biting racial slurs the choice expressions of the day within the sanctuary? Is it the automatic slashing edge during moments of anger and dissension generated by television or telephone, newspaper or neighbor? Is this self-fueling, self-renewing rage and disgust the sinister overpowering toxins of hate, and all that that signifies? Then what is the explanation for the same demeaning expressions and attitudes, and the racial identification and linkages, as expressed in public-and in anger or scorn-by the very young? What and who can be responsible for such racial awareness and precocity in the minds and mouths of the little ones and older youths? Is it the home? Is it family and friend? Is it the cocooning village?

It is customary to wax nostalgic that a whole village raises a child. It is very true, and this writer can attest firsthand to such experiences and truths. Even during the turmoil of what was labeled "disturbance" and "riot time" the village, with very few exceptions, groomed and guided, regardless of ethnicity. It worked, did wonders; and for this there is celebration and gratitude.

Now the same challenge is thrown at the feet of today's villages and the guiding elements: Dare to try practicing and living the old way! Try such with one's own and brace self; worse yet, attempt that across the racial divide. The result would highly likely be a furious, menacing blast from child, and a more furious confrontation from parent. This is a snapshot, a wide lens one, as to how polarized this society has become; as to how prolific such conduct is; as to how lacking in the rudiments is the new racial norm; and how acceptable it is too.

Next, ruminate for a moment on that most delicate and explosive of developments: youthful interracial romance; romance that culminates in eloping or hasty unions or an illegitimate child. This is sacred territory, and wounds deeply. From an Indian standpoint, this is the pits: a shame in the family, a wide dark stain of humiliation. There are some Indian parents who have disowned their erring children, especially daughters, and still have not spoken to them after decades of ostracism. The fortunate ones experience the partial mending of temporary reconciliations necessitated by terminal illness, death, or funerals. Forgiveness (for what?) is too many times not an option; so scorching and paralyzing are the memories of cultural and self-inflicted disgrace. The lost years cannot be retrieved; the damage is done at several levels: family, grandchildren, in-laws, community. The strong feelings triggered by race ripple silently outward across place and time. They do not heal.

From a Black perspective such romantic attachments are tantamount to steeping out of bounds, venturing into hostile territory, abandoning one's own, and consorting with the enemy. If anything, the emotions and reactions are less crippling, more muted, and manageable on the Black side. If there is anger, it is overcome more quickly. There is less cultural overload and almost nonexistent caste consciousness with which to battle. The journey is relatively easier. But all around there is discomfort and degrees of unhappiness that go beyond the usual tensions generated by same race partnerships. It is telling.

Staying in the homes tells other stories. It is that Indian and Black Guyanese look at separate TV channels, particularly those that peddle an embraced or embraceable political line, and subtle racial angles. They read different newspapers, again favoring those that cater to their partisan postures. Each hear and interpret the same news and developments radically differently; the controversial issues of the times are only viewed through heavily tinted telescopes –racial telescopes.

Moreover, the pleas of depressed Black communities are greeted with Indian scorn and skepticism in the form of: "is how much freeness dese people want fuh get?" And "wha it gun tek fuh satisfy dem?" Not to be outdone, the Black citizen is suffused with his own disdain and disbelief: "Is how much deh gun teef?" And "how long dis lawlessness gun guh aan?"

Also, there are some broad generalizations that have gained traction regarding the management of power: it is that Indians can manage a business, but not a country; make for good farmers but poor rulers. Then, there is the belief that Black people cannot run a cake-shop, and will run most things, most times into the ground. Both groups fear the thought and reality of the other holding the reins of power. It brings a shudder and lasting dread.

Within the social realm, one side condemns multiple teenage pregnancies, and single parenthood; the other damns the casual disregard for the sanctity of life through easy resort to clandestine abortions. From both blocs, and in large numbers, there emanates reciprocal moral disgust over what is viewed as chronic lapses. At the same level, there is acute distaste for the rum drinking orgies, musical depravity, sexual debauchery, suicidal solutions, and homicidal tendencies manifested by the other half. What is abhorred in the other is sometimes condoned in the fold.

Now look at religion and it will be noticed that nothing is sacred, nothing off-limits. There is contempt for some religious celebrations –as in Diwali. There is anxiety and bewilderment over African drums, garb, and practices. God, in all of his forms, loses ground when crimes with racial ingredients-victims and perpetrators-are brought to the forefront. People identify first with their own people who stand accused of perpetrating some criminal act; or are too muted and slow in the support extended to complaining victims; victims who worshipped under the same roof, and were accepted as brothers. Race trumps god, and religion is exposed as lacking in compelling virtues, to the detriment of Christian ethos, and what is right and wrong. This has coalesced into revivified racial disenchantment-sometimes within particular denominations-and solid distrust on numerous fronts. It as if there is no place that is clean and pure and resolutely color-blind. So even in the sacrosanct jurisdiction of prayer and worship, there is a forced bonhomie and superficial camaraderie, which retreats to defensive racial basements at the first sign of stress and conflict. It is just the way things are, and the way we are, for the most part.

The phrase "for the most part" functions as a meager, necessary qualifier. How so?

It is because amidst the tensions of the times, and the ugliness of barely concealed racial strife, there are the lustrous stories of crossover relationships, of color blindness when and where it counts; and of racial respect, understanding, and brotherhood. The problem is that these stories and occurrences are far too few, these genuine testimonies that have weathered time, overt and covert pressure, and all manner of circumstances imaginable. They are of good neighbors, enduring friendships, and bonds the near equivalent of blood relationships. If only there was a sizable nucleus, an influential bloc of such citizens, then this country would be a better place, and filled with the bright promise of tomorrow. But it is haphazard and accidental, more a matter of rare individual chemistry, than any practiced outreach, ennobling ideals, or shared vision.

It is why Guyanese are found exploitable and are exploited by racist politicians. This is never more obvious than before, during, and after national elections. Then the façade shatters, and the real truth surfaces.

National Elections: Lessons in Racial Hypocrisy

It is always a season of sharp unremitting tension; of verbal coarseness, of mental and emotional upheaval; and of *de facto* racial partitioning. There is the veneer of watchful civility, and palpable spacing between the races struggling for political supremacy. In this struggle, losing is deathlike; it means from both the Indian and Black standpoint, that one group's success equals failure for the other; that the opportunity for prosperity for one leads to the reality of poverty for the other; that the political ascendancy of winners translate to the racial doghouse for losers. In short, the triumph of one color heralds the devastation of the other. Yes, it is this punitive.

Because so much is at risk, these electoral contests have been knockdown, drag out affairs. For a certainty, there is some adherence to the political correctness of the times. But political correctness has facilitated the worst kinds of deception, hypocrisy, doublespeak, and cover. Messages are veiled, to which listeners are attuned; the postures are porous, and audiences sense this too. There are the patented hypocrisies-mainly for the record-about unity, democratic processes, concerns, issues, and visions. These are the mother and father of all farces; it is the biggest fraud and joke around, since nobody-be they politician or supporter-believes any of the copyrighted bull dung making the rounds.

89

Vote hustlers and captive voters know that, when all the shouting and assaulting are over, this is about one thing and one thing only: RACE! Do not stay home. Do not desert the clan. Do not give the other side a toehold. Do not trust them to look out for you and yours. Thus, all the old stereotypes, instigated misperceptions, and fierce distrust raise their Gorgon countenances under bottom houses, at street corners, and in community centers to rattle the ancient powder keg of racial fears, misgivings, and animosities.

There it is; there is no other thinking. There is no other way; there has been no other reality. The chief political players do not intend for it to be any other way. This is why those same leaders and their cronies hedge and deceive publicly, then turn right around and goad the faithful and uncertain into action through use of the flea-bitten, dog eared, race card. AND THEY DO USE IT PRODIGIOUSLY AND UNASHAMEDLY!

This is the steaming milieu of elections in Guyana. What place could there be for racial harmony when the loser is left with nothing but anger, disappointment, bitterness, hostility, even hate? When racial voting is encouraged and there is the refreshing of remembrances of perils and evils-old and new-in the hearts of racial constituents and other supporters? What chance harmony? How can this defused? How can this temperament, way of life, and turbulent atmosphere be eliminated and made a thing of the past?

None of this has a chance of happening as long as there continues to exist the helplessly divided adversarial racial camps. Camps that speak around each other, above each other, behind each other, and about each other in foaming torrents of words, and unending cacophonies of disaffection and distrust; The result is that the races never-repeat never-speak to each other in openness and through something approaching honesty. At the center, this is the naked exposed buttocks of racial and social communication and acceptance in this country. All of this is enabled, to different degrees, by crafty leadership, blind tribal allegiance, and the memory of history. It kills this society every time; the death is lingering and tortured.

In Guyana, election time assumes all the gut tightening, throat clogging, mind freezing promise and actual state of war. The major race-based political parties, and their racially motivated supporters, go on a war footing. For in the first place, losing could mean exposure, opening of books, and revealing of criminal conduct; this has led to desperation and antics that reek of the frantic. In the second place, losing the quadrennial political clash of arms leaves all the detritus of numbness of the spirit and shattering of the will in the aftermath. Just like real war, and lethal conflict, there is the haze and silence that amounts to what to do now? From here to where? What is left? And just as in real conflict, when there is a cessation of hostilities, there are usually guerillas in the remote bush, and saboteurs on the loose in the midst.

In 2012, political groups in particular, and the nation in general, have been the witness to, and objects of, a new kind of brinksmanship and political saber rattling. It is called "Snap Elections." Call it a trial balloon, a warning, a threat, a weapon, a joke, or an invitation. However viewed, it is all of these and then a smidgen more.

At the heart of the matter, these rumblings coming exclusively from the ruling PPP represent preemptive notice to fence sitting, rebellious, abstaining Indian voters. The word is: Stand up and be counted! Le t your votes be the difference. Now that these vacillators have the flames of Linden, and the mayhem of Agricola as evidence of the incorrigible characteristics of the opposition and its supporters, the time is ripe for them to get off their hands and do something. Like voting (for the Indian PPP, of course) and removing this albatross of a one seat parliamentary majority.

Certainly, resisting conscientious Indians do not need-could do without-the national humiliation of another tongue lashing from that self-elevated panjandrum who believes it is the right of the PPP to claim-no, demand-the voting birthright of its Indian constituency, regardless of its conduct while in office. Or to put it more crudely, but pointedly: It is the sacred duty of Indians to "keep the Black man out and keep the Indian man in." At all costs, or prepare to pay the consequences.

For its part, the studiously detached Black leadership believes that its supporters are sufficiently incensed to move beyond the polls, any kind of polls, to express wrath in the form of: "Dis craas gah fuh stap. Dis caan guh aan..." And "we ready fuh rumble, really rumble... Bring on yuh snap election. Bring it down!"

In summary, these are the reciprocal racial misperceptions and chronic disaffections that are always present to catapult the willing and the rash into action and at each other's throats. This is the state of racial disharmony that has existed in Guyana for the longest while, it grows in spiking temperature with the passage of time, and time only increases the clamor in the brain and impatience of the hand. These are not comforting thoughts; they imbue with dread. They point to where this nation is, and where it is straining to go. Now for some more hard, pointed questions: Are there any in Guyanese society who can make a difference? Are there some amongst the peoples who genuinely seek to carve out another way, a more constructive, inclusive destiny? Are these men and women-if they really exist-seen and accepted as catalysts for a different today and a new tomorrow?

CHAPTER VIII

TROUBLING TRUTHS: OF CIVIL SOCIETY, VOCAL MINORITIES, THE AFC, MONEY AND THE CHURCHES

"I believe in the sacredness of a promise, that a man's word should be as good as his bond, that character-not wealth or power or position-is of supreme worth."
-John D. Rockefeller Jr.

What about the socially respectable and sometimes well-regarded patriots? What about those who form part of the pillars of Guyanese life, and grace its roof gardens, who give every impression of involvement and concern? What of those who speak fluently-at times persuasively-of partnership and togetherness and lifting society up and out of the racial morass for the national good? When genuine durable change is so desperately needed do they have what it takes to be real agents for real change? What does this mean for the struggling, debilitated populace of whatever color in this man eat baby world? What likelihood is there for the stirrings of racial trust, and the tentative grasp of racial harmony?

Beware of Guyanese Politicians Bearing
Gifts (and those who accept)

They claim to be agents for improvement, but more than a few of them are compromised; they wax smartly of influencing change from the "inside" but nobody believes them. They think that they have covered their tracks, but they are wrong. They have mortgaged themselves, and with that comes political liability. At heart they are sensible people, and mean well, but they have an agenda that is more about the personal, and less of the national. For they serve more than one master, have their feet in two boats, and wear multiple hats –some known, some unknown.

Upon closer scrutiny, it will be found that they have treasured, lucrative links with the very abomination that has savaged this land and its peoples. Guyanese have an old saying: "Show me your company ..." Call it guilt by association, the reasonable man rule, or whatever; but it speaks for itself. A man can condemn the state of society, as afflicted by the scourges of drugs and drug merchants, but if his personal, professional, and business links are with these same magnates, then there is not much left to be said about him or his public utterances. Now substitute politicians for drug merchants and the picture should become very clear, as to who stands where.

This is how the rich, but buried, safety deposit box of association exposes the lack of authenticity and honesty in the publicly expressed concerns and interest of some. Others would rather forget that when gifts are artfully extended in this country by the ruling party, and accepted by seduced targets, it is the equivalent of the kiss of death. Say goodbye to credibility, and to stature. These gifts to old heads 'running the ward' can be a directorship, a ranking position, medical care, a job for a relative, a money grant, a piece of land, forestry or mining concession, or any similar such inducements. The die is cast in these veritable buy-and-bust operations, where secret loyalty is bought and independence (including integrity) busted. The recipients are now owned; and they are never allowed to forget. Also, they have forsaken their own credibility at the altar of money and personal advancement; and they have furnished a glimmer of longed for credibility to the political donors.

Has this not been the sordid record? Now how can these same folks-some professional people, some society people-speak for the common people when

94

they sup at the devil's table? Again, what credence can be given to warm and glowing public postures that embrace working together, when they are all about themselves? Is anyone listening to them? Should anyone do so?

Look at thyself first. Those who refuse to do so can be assured that the nation is scrutinizing them, and very critically, too. What has been sacrificed? Where is the self-denial? Where and who and what are the priorities? If the records indicate-and they do-that it has been first for self, then all the smooth, sweet talk about doing good are just that: smooth to the feel and sweet to the ear. But not anymore; because such unctuous words and postures are empty, empty of both intent and of possible fulfillment. They exemplify the platitudinous and the hypocritical.

If there is readiness to start from scratch with a clean slate then, of necessity, there must be a distance from those elements and forces that have harmed this nation. And there is no more tangible manner, no more convincing way than by rejecting the Grecian fruits and rewards offered to purchase person and reputation. Then a start can be made with those who care, who feel the pain of the suffering people, who understand and identify with the disillusionment. And the burning anger emanating from racial distress.

Infiltrating and Undermining the Well-meaning

Similarly, apolitical organizations (NGOs they are called) have been infiltrated by rank opportunists and an underground PPP Fifth Column. This is how a government obsessed with control keeps its ear to the ground: Comradeship is portrayed, friendships then betrayed, and ethics abandoned. Even Afro-centric bodies have been invaded. It is a sorry tale of Guyana. It is a prolific one that does considerable harm.

The work of well-meaning bodies is compromised, sold down the river to government buyers. There is a deep pool of funds and always an opportunity available for those with something to sell, and who have something for themselves uppermost in mind. In other words, the calculating, the weak, the vacillating, and the ambitious have a place and people waiting to make them feel welcome in the money store and job bank of the ruling party. Call it Judas unveiled. These are the new "insiders" and they are about as believable as those who like to say that they remained on the inside in an effort to influence change. The question is: change for whom?

What the ruling party is unable to obtain through human intelligence, it gathers through the presence in this place of surveillance cameras and secret intelligence units. Some of the latter might be so super-secret as to be completely unknown by anyone outside of rarified ruling circles. But among the nefarious purposes served are the introduction of fear, and the first tremors of increasing hesitancy. From the record, it can be gleaned that this entire expensive complex has done little, if anything, to solve burgeoning crime, which raise the questions: Why not? What are the true reasons for its presence? What mischief is the ruling party and government executing? Is it to further divide and rule? Is it to know more than is legally allowed? Is it to compromise regular citizens, and then control them along racial lines for racial purposes? The situation involving "vocal minorities" has supplied some grist for the mill of rumination.

Vocal Minorities –A Gravely Troubling Truth

Rather unwittingly, the PPP brass has substantiated some of what was stated earlier. Remember that much bandied about statement "vocal minority" and its cousins "opposition media" and "government critics?" Examine the former more carefully. For the first time in a long time, the PPP has uttered something approaching truth. Yes, it is accurate to say that there is a "vocal minority." In fact, it is the minority among local minorities, arguably the only real one. How so? It is because the government through subterfuge and infiltration has purchased, compromised, intimidated, and overpowered the majority into the prudence of silence and withdrawal. People are afraid, they retreat into anonymity, they settle for the valor of silence. End of story. Well not quite, for while this is true on the critical political side, there is a companion story on the **investigatory side,** which reveals how compromised and interlocking this society is at all levels; and how fear-stricken it is, too. It is where each level drifts right back into the political and the racial morass.

In late January 2013, there was a news story buried in the middle of a *Stabroek News* weekday edition. It was reported that police officials assigned to investigate high profile executions are reluctant-indeed, afraid-to pursue cases beyond superficial inquiry and going through the early motions. They are fearful for the safety of themselves and their families. It is a legitimate fear, which says several things simultaneously; and each of which is dangerous, if not lethal.

First, there is the hidden, though known, race factor in these types of killings: who ordered, who implemented, who fell? Second, it is clear that these killings involve more than gang warfare, and personal feuds. It is about business, and business has a significant racial DNA. Third, the common racial compositions of these three separate spheres of action (sponsors, perpetrators, and victims) were already raised and discussed: They are mainly brown, black, and black respectively. Fourth, some supposedly upstanding citizens have quietly denounced the publicly stated positions of those others who dared to say that this is a very lawless and corrupt society. Well, now here it is from members of the Guyana Police Force/Service themselves: They are fearful; they infer that their fear is from "out there" and is traceable to way "up there." They know. Ultimately, what the police said in not so many words is that footprints in high profile, unsolved murders point to high level circles; likely moneyed circles and commercial circles. By extension, though perhaps inadvertently, this identifies the racial complexion of local tribal politics. Now think through the implications of police hesitancy and fears, and discern where they lead. Think the dangerous nexus of commerce, crime, and color, then go from there. Some assistance is provided; it is probably not needed.

Police sleuths, without knowing it, illuminated the race angle and edge in deadly, high profile killings. There is the widespread belief that many of the local godfathers of crime are closely associated with the political administration, have supported it, and are protected by it. AND THAT THIS GROUP IS DOMINATED BY INDIANS, who are untouchable. Everybody believes this, knows this, and accepts this, including the police. In effect, this means that the men giving hefty political donations, hobnobbing with the brass, and offered as the epitome of local progress and development could be among the same men ordering hits and executions. Once again, the pointed lance of politics, race, and crime is drilled into the center of consciousness. It is a lance that discloses much under the full glare of closer scrutiny. The interconnectivity, no matter how disguised or distant or denied, is just there. This is taking matters where they have not been taken before: The GPF is not fearful of street shooters; these men are too busy running and hiding. The police ranks are fearful of the bosses who can arrange for others to blow people away, or eliminate interference; and from which nothing will come, or ever comes. Such is the strength of their connections and protections. Case closed.

What does this have to do with fear, withdrawal, and a shrinking vocal minority? It is this and it is rather ominous.

What is there to prevent these criminal godfathers to take care of the disobedient, the recalcitrant, and the vocal, given the auspices of the proper political wink and nod? How about doing a favor for the team? What about casually removing a noisy nettlesome presence, even if not asked, but thought to be problematic? What is one more? Who will care enough to do anything? Who would dare to challenge such a final solution? These are the rational concerns that emanate from the accumulated record of all these unsolved executions, and now publicly stated police apprehensions. Citizens use to fear-and fear even more now-speaking freely on the telephone. Nowadays they are concerned about who can silence them once and for all time, and without any consequences. So they express less. After all, policemen have already said that they are fearful.

The disbelieving are presented with the unsolved murder of Alicia Foster, the unsolved CLICO related shooting in Lombard Street, and the still unsolved disappearance of a conscientious public servant in 2012. These three examples reiterate that matters of this nature are not about low-level shooters and kidnappers in masks and white getaway Toyotas, but of the godfathers who gave them orders through trusted intermediaries. These godfathers could be men who circulate at the higher levels of society; and who are touted as model entrepreneurs. For those who like the bigger picture, recall Waddell and Sash Sawh, and then check for fingerprints.

To connect the dots further, recall that incident at the Leonora Police Station, where a teenager was brutally tortured. Officials of the law broke the law because they surmised that such would go down well with the political masters, given the identity of the murdered victim. They were doing a favor. Taking this a step higher, the local 'big fishes,' would have no qualms doing what they believe to be desired-but unstated-political favors, just like the Leonora torturers; it is part of the business necessity of the bigger boys.

Who would care for too long over the passing of a critic or an agitator? If law enforcement officials worry that they could be targeted in attempts to solve murders, then who is safe? With a stricken law enforcement apparatus, silence might be the only option, other than for the brave or the utterly foolish. And nobody who is minimally sensible seeks to be the latter. It is why the vocal minority grows less loud, and less populated daily; and more cautious, too. It picks safe subjects: criminal racial connections and the implications are not among them. It is just one more troubling truth in today's Guyana —one that could prove to be gravely so. Literally.

Now it is time for some thoughts on the loudest, most visible minority of them all —the AFC.

AFC: Third Force or Fifth Wheel?

The Alliance for Change ("AFC") when it first emerged from the shadows of the two major parties and burst on the scene appeared to be the longed for "Third Force," change agent, and difference maker. It has disappointed. Its initial vision and strategy did not extend to that of grassroots mobilizer when it arrived. Precious time and ground were lost in that introductory moment. For too long, it contented itself with being armchair activists and media generals; it lacks broad based appeal now, and is not viewed as a catalyst for change. Now, the newcomer is increasingly bogged down in a PPP dictated and dominated world; and is entangled in all manner of peripherals, red herrings, and too many other ruses, some of which are self-created.

Second, some of-much of—the AFC's failure to make a significant impact and its resulting stagnation is traceable to the powerful influence and stranglehold that the PPP and PNC have on their respective ethnic bases. This incalculable influence and stranglehold encompasses racial consciousness, racial loyalty, racial fears and racial immobility; it leads to the expected reflexive racial response every time. It is the equivalent of stick with the program as known. No change. Another way of looking at the relationship between party and follower is through understanding what happens to those abused and beaten (usually the woman) daily by a troubled partner. On the rare day that she is not abused and beaten, she is lost and doesn't know what to do, and thinks that something is wrong. It is a part of her resigned, numbed state of normalcy. The case can be made that despite the chronic abominations of the PPP and PNC, their battered supporters do not know of life without them; will not consider a new beginning. This is the AFC's loss.

Third, the records indicate that none is more obdurate in adhering to this history than Indo-Guyanese. They certainly did not migrate to the AFC in any substantial numbers (even with Moses) during its still brief presence. Perhaps they fell for the PPP propaganda that the AFC was the PNC by another name, and it was a backdoor attempt by the latter to sneak its way into power; maybe they were fearful and distrustful. It could be that Indians will cling to the PPP no matter what, and that the farthest they will venture is to the point of momentary absence and abstention. The PPP is their retarded child, their profligate, their degenerate. Said differently "nobady gah baad bush fuh troweh." Also, there is the fear that piercing the nose could permanently disfigure the face. While a few Indians listened and questioned their consciences, fewer are moved to act, and to turn their backs on the PPP. That would be racial treason and unpardonable. Additionally, Indians did not embrace ROAR with any degree of enthusiasm or great numbers, despite its openly stated prioritization of Indian interests and welfare. It is likely that they saw such action as dilutive to PPP strength and power, and contributory to PNC resurgence. If Indians will not migrate to ROAR, then they are not going anywhere else.

In terms of its composition, the AFC has attracted as of late, some high profile names and faces. They help and hinder. There is concern in some quarters that men are so politically ambitious that they will explore any avenue, consort with any available friend (or enemy), and play any game to achieve their personal agendas. There is the belief that if offered the right positional inducement, they will abandon ship. Of course, there will be the unpersuasive justification of 'influencing change from the inside' to sugarcoat such rank opportunism. The most printable thing that could be said of such rationale is that it stinks. Further, there are some who bring baggage involving conduct unbecoming and rising to the level of obstruction of justice, serious obstruction. This speaks for itself.

The result is that both Indians and Blacks look at the AFC and see considerable reasons as to why they should avoid aligning with the party. On its own, the AFC allows itself to be suckered into multiple distractions and end up spread too thin, not identified with anything, and solving nothing. Its thinking and tactics are self-enfeebling, and reduces its role to that of heckler, rather than that of a force with which to be reckoned. Thus, the political and racial continuum extends unchecked, unbalanced, unchallenged, and unchallengeable. It is helped considerably by the presence of oceans of easy dirty money.

The Role of Money

What follows is not related to corruption. Rather, it is provide an idea of how much 'play' money is available for political contributions and, by extension, political and racial mischief.

It is well known that large segments of the new "middleclass" and the arriviste private sector are overloaded with easy money looking for a home. It is widely believed that they have been generous in sharing the dirty fruits of their endeavors in substantial amounts with the ruling party. Read dollars and by the suitcase; then pick a currency. It is possible that, despite the towering shrines and staggering overnight opulence that abound, most Guyanese are not truly familiar with the vast, oceanic sums of dirty cash that pour into this country through a multiplicity of fronts, some of which is earmarked for political sponsorship. Real killings, and possible high political crimes, have been committed under the auspices of a generous cascade of such funds. This is money that helps to facilitate tawdry political practices and intensifies racial fear and loathing.

To gain an appreciation of the presence and role of dirty money in Guyana, consider the following not so well known outline. The dirty laundering arrangements start at fifty cents (or thereabouts) on the U.S. dollar: that is the amount to be repatriated to the foreigners supplying the money; the last fifty cents stay with the natives here. Now consider that the "seed money" amounts to only several hundred thousand such dollars at the inception of the relationships, when trust is developed. Then extend the amounts pouring in locally to the millions, as confidence grows. In total, this represents a lot of 'fifty cents' for doing nothing, other than functioning as fronts and proxies. At an exchange rate of 200:1 some picture should emerge as to the astronomical amounts flooding the Guyanese street, and overflowing local coffers. It is unimaginable, almost immeasurable; so it is a no-brainer to give lavishly to political protectors, who make so much possible. It is part of the cost of doing business.

Next, think of imports arriving in this country by the shipload and container. Then, consider the duty evaded, which could routinely run into seven figures, but is still embedded in the final price paid by the public. So it is profit upon profit. Also, opportunities are manufactured to commingle dirty money with clean money. That is, for each dollar of legitimate proceeds, there is another twenty more deposited as normal business takings. But there is more.

At a rate of sixteen percent, VAT is part of the yoke that chokes the poor Guyanese consumer; it is not discriminatory. VAT, however, functions as yet another source of rich profiteering for the celebrating class. How so? Through the maintenance of two sets of books, and the delivery of a fraction of the tax collected to the national treasury. **Care is taken to point out again that this is NOT about corruption and sleaze.** Rather, it is a fast-moving outline of the money machine-and its sources-that enables the feeding of the political monster, and facilitates all that follows to the detriment of the majority, and particularly working-class Black Guyanese.

In combination, the laundry industry, the import duty partnership arrangements, and the VAT withholdings, all point to stupendous sums of cash available for any nefarious purpose whatsoever. This has included political purposes, which translates to continuing racial discord, through extending Indian hegemony, and exacerbating Black distress.

Which politician in this country is principled enough, patriotic enough, and care for the struggling masses enough to say "NO!?" Which ruling politician, come election season, would turn back a bulging sugar bag of cash? Especially when there is complete awareness that such unsolicited donations could well find their way to political foes, if refused?

And so the unchanging story continues: fun and games on one side with one racial beneficiary; need and distress on the other for racial losers. This is the stuff that powers social upheaval of the worst sort. Men have said repeatedly that the ruling party is going to get burned, and burned badly. The problem is that there are vulnerable people in the middle who will experience the brunt of the heat, become the dry statistic and drier euphemism of "collateral damage." It is a primer for tragedy, and there is nothing in the middle to cushion.

The Lack of a Genuine Local Buffer

Taken together, these blocs (private sector and new middle class) are negligible and formidable outposts that stand against the rising tide of rancor. Formidable because each provides considerable material and philosophical support towards the maintenance of the status quo; and negligible because they are seen for what they really are: hypocritical, self-serving, and hostile to change. They lack credibility, as they are not seen as principled, trustworthy intermediaries and brokers. In spite of determined efforts to erect a stealth screen, they are part of the political vulgarity, and very much so.

For their part, civil society groups, and other likeminded entities operate under severe handicaps. They mean well, the calls are ringing, but there are no takers. They discuss and strategize *ad infinitum*, but action sleeps at the table of discussion and concern; it refuses to rise, or be roused.

Further, there is no buffer race or bloc between the two antagonistic races, which together constitute close to eighty percent of the population. The two races are too numerically dominant, too concentrated, too close to each other, too mutedly hostile to each other for intervening local strains-and strains they are-to be an effective cushion for the omnipresent racial animus. Local buffers, such as indigenous or mixed groups, are too insignificant in numbers and influence to be recognized and accepted as difference makers. They have not been up to this date, and the future is expected to be the same. They are present, but do not count; they can be seen, but are not heard. They are recognized as mere pawns to be tricked, maneuvered, and purchased into conditional, temporary loyalty, and are viewed as both divided and hopelessly compromised.

All that is left is so much bad blood: There is too much surrounding racial sickness on both sides from the leaders at the top right through to those at the bottom immersed in distrust, anxiety, and despair. Yes, there is just too much dirty history that will not let go, and too much of a sharp present that further entangles.

These are the circumstances that push local moderates to the sidelines; their public numbers diminish, and so does their influence, including the so-called Portuguese Mafia. Enter the wired radicals, the hair trigger militants, and the short-fused extremists; it is the hour of "wild men" and "dangerous men." Caution is abandoned, straws are clutched, and the odds are ignored.

When people are sufficiently disturbed and outraged over everyday excesses at the hands of the domineering state, they then whip themselves into a state of constant hostility, and are ready to be driven-or initiate-extremes of action. In such times, the simmering, resentful masses-in this case racially segmented-are ripe for recruiting, ready to be unleashed, and prepared to destroy and to kill. And be killed. The consequences do not matter. What is there to lose?

Divided societies are always at high risk for such upheavals; where a group believes itself ostracized, demonized, and victimized it cares little for civility and restraint in the long run. It will fight; it will trash decency as an artificial construct that serves the interest of the contented, and which shackles the energies, bottles the fears, and stills the anger of the impoverished and downtrodden. Guyana is no exception. There is growing evidence that local conditions have been in this dangerous state for some time now; it keeps intensifying ....

Churches: Conflict between the Spiritual and the Racial

While in the depressed environments of compromised respectable society, weakened civil society, government secret surveillance society, and racial criminal society, it is time to wander over into the realm of the church. How does religion and god fare in Guyana? How do both measure up in the scheme of racial impressions and calculations?

It was Karl Marx who wrote that, "Religion is the opium of the people." While there might be some truth to this statement, religion is one dope that has been neutralized, and then conquered in Guyana. Effortlessly. In Guyana, worshippers, including the committed and devout, bow down first in the sanctuary of race; it is the most sacrosanct of shrines. Religion and belief-however denominated-take a back seat, is relegated to distant second place. God is given a mandatory holiday, and so, too, are all the attendant standards during crunch times and crises. This is never more evident than during election season, when the hysteria powered racial wagons are circled. Closet racial veterans and vibrant racial warriors emerge from under their religious cowls and ecclesiastical hiding places; they hold the racial banner aloft in the glorification and adoration of what is dearest to their hearts. They are not subtle.

During these usually testing and turbulent times, god is secondary, god is color, and god is me and mine first. All the inspiring brotherhood of peace and love, the karma of goodness, and the blindness of faith disintegrates on the anvil of racial priorities and the fundamentalism of racial aspirations. Individuals of usually commendable religious profundity and grace, who can make urgent and vital contributions to watching brethren and larger society, are lost to the siren call of racial allegiance. They cannot help themselves; they refuse to take a stand for truth and right. All the doctrines and commandments amount to naught.

Those who had "crossed over" to the Christian faiths question themselves on the godliness of what is observed; as to what transformed these brothers and sisters that they thought they knew so well; and the significance of the new revelations. The answers are obvious and disturbing: race and politics in the narrowest, ugliest Guyanese senses of the two words. The reflexive thoughts for believers are best summarized in this way: What am I doing here? I do not belong here. I should not be here where the Prince of Peace and the Good Shepherd is mocked.

On the other hand, there is little such internal conflict and remonstrations in the non-Christian sectors. The guiding scripture is simple: All for One! It is the rapture of "Our Time. Our Turn." All the harm and injury, all the wicked deeds, all the vile excesses fade into oblivion. Truth and uprightness and ethics-inclusive of religion ones-do not matter. Race matters. Nothing else does, including god. These are the crucibles in which the Indian and Black faithful are ensnared; they study each other and do not like what they see, and what they judge. The practices and results condemn both for failure to adhere to the best traditions and dogmas incorporated in their belief systems.

When even organized religion is conveniently, effortlessly jettisoned in favor of racial preference, then the last comforting refuge is gone. When there are no spiritual bulwarks left to shield, then each is on his own. It is but one more troubling truth here in Guyana.

Once again, the question raised earlier is revisited: What does the local environment reveal as to support for, or dismissal of, the believed promise of the future? That is, in terms of what it encompasses in racial rift, fear, discontent, hostility, and the dire need for change and reinvention. This is what the environment reveals.

It is that the poor are on their own, and have to look out and take care of themselves. It is that racial dangers-meaning Black dangers-can be minimized, even nullified. It is that there will be no voluntary, ground-breaking change. In fact, there will be no change at all. Period. According to the ruling clique, things are just lovely the way they are. Smarter men have made lesser miscalculations and paid a steeper price. Usually, it is the ordinary citizen, the man-in-the-street who pays that terrible price. Men and women will pay that price here, for there is no buffer to separate or dilute or redirect; no arbiter ready to intervene; no factor that can influence positive change.

Hence, Guyanese, black and brown, trudge wearily through their palpably dreary days; sometimes friendly, mostly guarded; stoic in civility, muted in hostility. This is the cosmetic gloss of many fears, the encroaching threat of distant, sinister lightning flashes. There is the dullness of emotional despair, psychic decay, and a paucity of hope. Some leading churchmen in Europe said in 2012 that "hopelessness is the greatest of all evils." They are right; simply ask poor, struggling Guyanese, and particularly Black Guyanese. At the end of the day, all the anger, all the hostility, all the frustrations will crescendo in that fateful chant of: "No justice, no peace!"

Highly Overblown or Hugely Understated?

It is possible that quite a few citizens-intelligent, thoughtful, and patriotic-would find all of this too much to stomach. They might view this as alarmist, provocative, even inflammatory in content and nature. They look around and pronounce themselves comfortable with what they see, and with the way things are. They see what they want to see, and there is some basis for their complacency. Take a look.

The comfortable and unconvinced watched as an ugly, dangerous situation-a potentially substantial health hazard-developed in the vicinity of the Le Repentir cemetery. Two well-known local activists decided that this warranted action and highlighting for public attention and reaction. They were promptly shackled and hauled off to jail. The result was that nobody said a word, raised a finger, or made a step towards the streets to protest on behalf of their volunteer advocates. Nobody! Why, even the folks in the neighborhood impacted the most, and who were likely to be imperiled further, did absolutely nothing for themselves or their defenders. Such is the level of malaise and apathy-call it whatever pleases-that prevails. None could be stirred to action for self-protection. None could be motivated to take a stand. None!

The good, smart people look at this and shake their heads in knowing confirmation: "See, nothing is going to happen. Nothing comes out of anything. Afire could be lit under the people, and they would not respond, not move. They don't care anymore; they have lost the ability to feel." Thus, they conclude somewhat smugly that all this talk of dissonance, uprising, and abyss is so much misplaced thinking and projection.

The same people notice the same lukewarm intensity and low level energy when there are repeated incidents of state killings, many of which are suspicious, if not downright criminal. Nobody rallies; nobody protests for too long. The sun is too hot, the street too flooded, the security too oppressive. It was the same half-hearted, feeble reaction when a number of individuals were shot with rubber pellets during a peaceful opposition protest march. It did not matter that senior men were injured; it was of little consequence that investigations were sloppy and follow-up proceedings deteriorated into the usual farce. This includes the ignominy of quiet routine dismissal in court; it was as if nothing had happened. Everyone had simply moved forward to other challenges of succeeding days.

Thus, the smirk from the disbelieving: "See there! If nothing erupted then, nothing is going to occur now. Not now, not anytime." This is the comforting conclusion of the well-cocooned, who make no waves —not even a ripple. They sense no anger, see no danger, share no concern. They are wrong, for many are the racial abscesses that have developed; they are inflamed, they hurt, and they drip ...

Indeed, this is a serious misreading of the powerful racial undercurrents that rage beneath the surface calm of this fragmented society. Those who prefer to retreat behind shaded windows and coated lens, and who are confident in their pretentions and forced ignorance, are playing with fire, and hoping against hope. They ignore those two loaded, oft referenced quotes herein, from the Speaker of the House and the president himself —quotes about "civil war" and "hate" and "haters." Failure to recognize debasing racial realities in this country for what they are, leads to grievous miscalculation, and perilous complacency. It also adds to the scorn and intransigence in ruling political circles. The end result is that there is a hardening of attitudes and postures all around.

In all of this, Guyanese forget the lessons of history. They forget-or refuse to remember-that when the downtrodden, disrespected, and degraded have their backs pushed against an unyielding wall, and their noses rubbed repeatedly in offal, they do the unthinkable and they respond through the unexpected. The despairing takes matters in their own hands, and seek outlet for their discontent and there ensues burning destructive wrath. It is that when people have nothing to hope for, nothing to lose, they hurl caution to the winds, and challenge the seemingly unbeatable foe. Perhaps the thread of something good might result. The collective groupthink is: Why listen? Why believe? Why wait? Why not act? Why not act now?

This is some of what the Linden community demonstrated to a watchful country. There was a sense of newfound strength, of tumultuous coalescence, and of gathering cohesion. There was a sense of purpose. And, of course, the entire enduring confrontation reopened unhealed wounds, and rekindled long held racial beliefs on both sides of the rift. It is an intrinsic aspect of the steeply downward road on which this nation journeys.

Then Agricola exploded with sharp, jarring suddenness in a boiling Gehenna of nocturnal violence. Every victim froze then rushed away with rancorous memories of racial assault that will endure for a lifetime; every onlooker came away with thoughts on the limitations, and ultimately the failure, of public institutions to stem the tide. AND ALL HAD THEIR EYEBALLS SEARED AS TO HOW THINGS REALLY ARE IN GUYANA. From the police shooting, to early community objection, to continuing state nonchalance, to that fateful word and phrase, and to the mayhem that followed, this timeline of events shredded the willful individual and political stupidity that clouds judgment, imbues with false confidence, and resists movement.

Further, there were palpable unsettling fears over rumored movements of another kind. There were reports of movements from the Linden Township to show solidarity with residents of Agricola; they were hazy apprehensions of mobilizations in Buxton. Together, they represented a possible pincer converging on the capital for the pressure of a powerful squeeze. Together, these three communities-overwhelmingly

Black-embody the anguish of one group, and the anxieties of the other. They are not three isolated, unattached communities; but the more visible collective manifestation of the simmering resentments that course through Black minds and Black life in Guyana.

TOGETHER THESE COMMUNITIES HAVE LAID BARE THE MASSIVE RIFTS THAT EXIST IN THIS UNBALANCED SOCIETY. Even if for the wrong reasons, and acted upon in wrong ways, it has to be undeniable that massive racial rifts exist, always did. Perhaps, they always will. The invariable result that follows and grows is stronger racial identification and allegiance; and extreme disaffection.

These lessons might be lost on those who force themselves-in the face of all the bleak daily realities-to imagine laughter and joy from those at the bottom of the pile, who wait for the gilded grains and silver scraps of handouts. The thoughtless might even hear echoes of cheer: "yes massa. Things good; everything real good." Nothing could be more distant from the truth; nothing could be any less indicative of the rage that sizzles, and the fires that burn. The unwilling ignore the violent examples raging outside of Guyana; the unhappy notice them.

PART III

The Prospects and Perils:
Whirlwinds in the Waiting

CHAPTER IX

A World of Violent Change ~Resisting Second Class Status

*"Is life so dear, or peace so sweet, as to be purchased at
the price of chains and slavery? Forbid it, Almighty God!"*
-Patrick Henry

There is stubborn, raging discontent. There is ongoing, violent resistance. And there is determined struggle and sacrifice to go the way of separation and independence. This is the life and times of minorities in quite a few places on this globe. Sometimes, it is a majority that is compelled to rise up and remove the shackles of oppression, the rule by another kind. The thinking is the same: many groups cannot-will not-live under conditions of resigned submissiveness, of perpetual inequality, and of a visionless circumscribed future for themselves. No matter how benevolent the rulers, how peaceful the circumstances (and usually they are not), members of the minority groups desire the freedom to be their own masters. They fight for this precious, sacred right. Usually, their fighting is violent and without adherence to conventions and rules.

Minorities: Rising, Rekindling, Resisting

Sometimes the troubled, rebellious minorities are numerically tiny, an ethnic pool in the larger majority sea, and their violent agitation is traceable to different reasons and priorities. It could be for the clan, the tribe, ethnicity, religion, even a particular ideology. But almost always the sharp, jabbing underpinnings are the same: poverty, marginalization, majority oppression, no voice, no meaningful representation, state indifference, state disrespect and scorn, state sponsored violence, and inequitable distribution of state resources, among other bitter grievances. Minorities press forward in determined effort to level the field, and to bring about wrenching change paid for in blood. They are driven by the indignity of deprivation, and infuriated by the stigma of wanting and coming up empty. Constantly. The vacillating middle and cowering moderates are seen as obstacles and swept out the way.

In many ways, these grievances mirror the perceptions, feelings, and realities that exist within segments of the Guyanese population. These are the perceptions, feelings, and realities of the majority poor, whether Black, Indian, or Amerindian; and none is more negatively impacted than Black Guyanese. Perception is fuel, it is blood, and it is fire.

Groups, wherever there may be-no matter how small, how well treated-are no longer content with minority status, and to exist in a second class state. This becomes clear in the quick and brief examples that follow shortly. These rebel groups are known and recognizable. They surely cause cringing and distaste when they surface with brutal suddenness in the news. But they epitomize the fierce unrelenting determination to answer the call within and rouse themselves into bloody resistance; to take a stand for going their own way; and to lay their lives on the line to carve out their own destiny. They do so in tactics and strategies that the comfortable and unconcerned consider barbaric and overflowing with sickening, gruesome savagery. It is the way chosen; many times it is the only way left. Here are some quick examples from elsewhere.

The Muslim Abu Sayyaf in the Philippines

Observe the Abu Sayyaf rebels in the Philippines. Much of the civilized world looks upon them as terroristic. They are miniscule in numbers —perhaps several hundred, certainly not many thousands. Their struggle and quest is in the name of religion; it is the independence of an Islamic state. This overwhelmingly Catholic country has long decided upon, and implemented, a military solution against this upstart minority, this vicious poisonous thorn. The people of Bastian Island, Moro and Mindanao are suspected of offering them shelter. For a long time, this drop-in-the-bucket presence in the Philippines resisted and struggled and inflicted horrific damage. That struggle is not fully settled.

The Ideological Naxalites of India

Take note of the Naxalites in India, the self-proclaimed world's largest democracy. They are a numerically more robust group, when compared to the Abu Sayyaf, but are still lost in the massive picture that is India. The Naxalites have some serious issues with that word called democracy; it means nothing to them, offers no succor. Their voices cry out about poverty and an uncaring central government. Their cries have been backed by unbelievable savagery in a continuing war against the mammoth state. They clamor and kill for the dream of a separate, independent existence away from under the shadow of distant masters. In a country of over a billion souls, the Naxalites fade into the background. But they refuse to be swallowed up; these wayward, backward "tribals" will not submit to their lot. They continue to fight.

Others Elsewhere: Slavs, Tamils, Uighurs, Chechens

It is the same story of dogged resistance, dreadful violence, and a search for freedom and peace in such flashpoints as Kashmir, Iraq, and Ireland. In those places, majorities have been denied for the longest time. The conflicts are imbued with a fanatical and fundamentalist bent. And though religion is the main ingredient, these convulsions have been about killing and more killing.

Here is the main thrust of these bloody, lethal conflicts: whatever the driving force —be it ethnic, religious, tribal, economic, or other-**groups, especially** minority groups, want out from under the yoke of connectivity. They do not want to be attached to the majority, to the oppressors, to the usurpers, to the different, or to the "other." They just don't want to live anymore under such an arrangement.

This was seen in what became of the old Yugoslavia, and which was reconfigured into Bosnia, Serbia, and Herzegovina. Horrific prices were paid in reciprocal atrocities, including a tragedy such as Srebrenica. In vast, unending China, the Uighurs seek recognition through self-determination and independence; they fear the encroaching presence of the majority Han Chinese in their Manchurian domain. They dread the loss of identification through ethnic inundation, thanks to state policy. Inevitably, the conflict has deteriorated into rising sporadic violence and a harsh, unforgiving stand-off. It is the same struggle and agitation with the Chechens in Russia.

And who can fail to remember Sri Lanka and the conflict there between the majority Sinhalese and minority Tamils, and the latter's push for separation? This was the rebel group that opened the eyes of the world to the physical lethality and psychological impact of the suicide bomber. It is a cheap, portable, terrifying, devastating one-man catastrophe. The means towards ends ....

All over the rebel war cry is the same: No to dominance! No to majority rule! No to belonging! No to submission! No to acceptance!

It goes without saying that all of this means "Yes to self-determination, to separation, and to independence. In the same instance, the majority-whoever it might be, and wherever it is-will not act. It refuses to give an inch; it is too set in its ways, too comfortable in its hegemony, and too mesmerized by the rewards of dominance. It wants things to remain as they are, have always been. These majorities are also contemptuous of the aspirations of impotent, despairing minorities in their midst. Hence, the response from the bottom-of-the-barrel, from the forests, and from the hearts of the denied has been unambiguous: unprecedented violence and terror. Horrendous. Remorseless. Unrelenting.

It should not escape the attention that not a word has been spared for the overused bandwagons of colonialism, divide-and-rule, tribal rearrangement, calculated racial juxtaposition, or geographical redrawing. These are all known, and regurgitated too often and too conveniently. None of this unravels the strands of history, or changes the reality faced today —it is what it is. Impacts yes; changes, no!

Guyana –Parallel or Exaggeration?

Guyanese live with this heritage –all of them. It hurts, it enfeebles, it paralyzes. It also angers and disturbs and divides. Thus, the peoples of this society do not go forward as a nation. They go forward as peoples, separate and distinct; resentful and joyful; triumphant and defeated. It does not inspire confidence in the present or continuity into the future.

They hear-already know-of all the examples highlighted in rushing detail above. They are familiar with the chilling ugliness of Rwanda. In the throes of their plight, Black Guyanese, in particular, unconsciously identify with the Nigerian writer Obafemi Awolowo who said, "Nigeria is not a nation. It is a mere geographical expression." And they associate with Abubakar Tafawa Balewa, later to become Prime Minister, when he said: "The Nigerian people themselves are historically different in their backgrounds, in their religious beliefs and customs and do not show themselves any willingness to unite ..."

It is submitted that the same can be said of Guyana and Guyanese; that it is representative of local reality; and that many hearts beat this way.

Now take a step from Africa to Europe and America for a couple of rapid strokes. Great Britain is not desirous of-is resistant to-immersion in the European Union. It seeks to preserve its identity. Across the pond, the inhabitants of Red Dog states have difficulty submitting to a Blue Dog leader, so much so that if secession was a feasible option, it might very well have been in the cards. The point is that even in advanced, wealthy, mature societies there is objection and resistance to absorption, or leadership of a different kind.

Whether Africa or Europe or America or Asia, the surging questions are these: If there, why not here? If where there is plenty (and plenty of history), why not here where is little or nothing? Again, no group desires to be lost in the mass, to be a mere statistic, or nothing more than a cypher. Or second best.

For a long time, these artificial constructs, this coerced environmental and social herding, have existed and prevailed in uneasy restlessness, and mainly muted turmoil. They have been held together by force of arms, trickery, and a philosophy called democracy. This democracy is, at times, what a whimsical, capricious majority says it is; it can be terribly unjust to those hovering beyond the reach of its nobler provisions. For all practical purposes and from bitter experience, democracy for minorities means consignment to the realm of the voiceless, the powerless, and the meaningless. And in Guyana, this points to racial disaster.

As if in confirmation, a very senior, sensitively placed public officer shared that when societies are highly polarized, conflict inevitably results. History has revealed that whatever the reason-ethnicity, economics, or equity, among others-violence is a foregone conclusion. It might not be the best example, but the emblem of the Jewish underground organization, Irgun, comes to mind: There were the words **"Thus Only"** accompanied by a raised right arm and a rifle with a bayonet attached. No explanation should be needed as to mindset and objectives. In addition, history has shown that, during such times of upheaval, constitutionally sanctioned forces move to restore order by taking control. Many times the leaders of those same stabilizing forces grow to like their newfound power, and convert it to a state of permanent oversight. This is an alien condition regionally, but it should be remembered that there were movements in this direction in neighboring Surinam and Trinidad several years ago. They stand as precedents that should not be dismissed.

Now some will rear up in strident protest and righteous indignation, at what they consider some form of sacrilege, of ignorance, of gross exaggeration. They should stop the pretense and be honest for once. Once again, they are reminded of those two words uttered by the Speaker of the House, when he talked about "civil war." And the president at Babu John who warned through his own two words about "hate" and "haters." And he was not talking of the AFC or deserters or vocal minorities. This is how real and raw and ugly matters are: civil war and hate. There is a fever developing amidst the many scattered outposts where resistance brews in the mind. There are guns everywhere: in the hands of hated overlords, underlings, the surrounding Palace Guard, and those who aspire to replace them. Guyana's situation is not an altogether dissimilar to nuclear tipped, neighboring archenemies India and Pakistan. Here, however, the boiling point is not religion, but race and history that sizzle. Though there are no weapons of mass destruction, there exist huge arsenals of weaponry on both sides to produce a domestic mushroom cloud. Such is the cataclysm that threatens. All it takes is a few committed sufferers to light the fuse, and to trigger a maelstrom.

The hard questions that confront one and all-the patriotic, the thinking, the conscientious, the political analyst, the racist, the partisan, and the visionary-are these: Is this not where we are? Is this not who we are? Is this not how we have been? How different are we from Nigerians or Kashmiris or Chechens? Emotions aside, and employing a detached and clinical approach, is this not reflective of the real Guyana at the racial core and deep in the psyche? When the silky pretensions to unity and oneness, understanding and the forced experience of wearisome tolerance are abandoned, is this not what exists? When the permeating physical, verbal, racial postures are revealed in all their ugliness, obscenity, injury, and lethality from over a half century ago, and in between, do they not undermine and smite national cohesion, and make a mockery of it? Can the same not be said of those postures that have been rekindled in the last two decades through increasing hostility and unbridled contempt?

When all things are considered, this is the real Guyana in varying degrees of intensity from pit to penthouse: suspicious, distrustful, contemptuous, and barely civil. It is a fragile existence that refuses to search for common bonds and grounds. That is, if there is any to be found, to be recognized, and to be embraced as such. Accordingly, all that is left is the specter of devastation brought about by wrenching violent change. And the tools to make such destruction possible are present in prodigious quantities. These tools go by the simple name of guns ....

CHAPTER X

GUNS ~THE ULTIMATE POWERBROKER

"Political power grows out of the barrel of a gun."
—Mao Zedong

Guns have become the final solution in Guyana. They are the instrument of choice to settle scores, to bring equilibrium to contests, and to dispense justice. The latter might be arbitrary, criminal, or political; the political usually means the racial. Guns will most likely be the deciding factor, the agent of change, and the ultimate arbiter given the atmosphere of racial animosity, the reality of racial division, and the presence of growing racial anger. Guns will determine if there will be peace, and what will follow. It is the height of macabre, lethal irony that guns will end up being the peacemaker; perhaps the harmonizer in this torn, hapless society. What a price to be paid for peace, for the possibility of a future, and for some semblance of decency and equity. Or perhaps, none of any of this.

Gun Massacres – A Handful Only

In Rwanda, the machete took the place of the Grim Reaper's arcing scythe; it was no less heinous or deadly in reach or result. Perhaps it was more so in terms of viciousness and victims; the barbaric release of pent-up fury and frustrations; a dam breached. Remember: there was no mercy, no exceptions; no free pass for sympathizers, for innocents, even for fellow tribesmen. In Guyana, guns stand to take the place of the machete. It is obvious that they already have, as was recently experienced with appalling frequency and horrific results. A good place to start would be February 23, 2002. Later, guns invaded Lusignan and mowed down in cold-blooded, calculated rage. None was spared –not women, not children, not babies. The victims were all adults from the continuing unprecedented savagery at Bartica and Lindo Creek. It was the same frightening story: guns and more guns. And it was the same during a rampage at Agricola, the attack on a Minister's residence, the assault at a PPP gathering in Rose Hall, and the resistance in Buxton. Yes, more guns; many, many guns.

Guns –The Search for a Number
(How many and for what purpose?)

Some questions must now be raised. The first is: How many guns are in the hands of Guyanese? Whether licensed or illegal, how many are there altogether out there? Since there can obviously be no definitive official record concerning illegal firearms, what is a reasonable approximation as to their number? Last, what does that number represent in terms of the potential to inflict devastation? Now some answers are offered.

At last count, and from public disclosure over a year or so ago, there were some 30,000 licensed firearms in the possession of citizens. By itself, this is a staggering number, which most likely has not shrunk, but increased. Using the convenient number of approximately 300,000 adults in this country, this equates to one gun for every ten adults. If the number is halved to 150,000 for males only, who are usually overwhelming in interest and actual ownership, then there could likely be one gun for every five adult males trolling the streets. It gives no comfort to know that some of the guns have been issued to doddering, untrained, cataract afflicted incompetents, from whom these dangerous toys are easily separated by the bad guys. Regardless of the actual numbers and final ratio, there are already too many guns in this society, **and this is from licensed firearms only.**

For a certainty, quite a few of these would be for legitimate reasons and lawful purposes; such as business and asset protection, and a recognized need for deterrence and self-defense. It could also be said with similar certainty that most of these licensed firearms have been issued to men with strong ruling party connections. For a moment, it appears that the scales are tilted; but only for a moment. For now comes the million dollar question, the second one, the real burning one: How many unlicensed and unaccounted for guns are there in this society? It does not matter whether these guns are in the cities or villages, with government or opposition supporters, in the hands of criminals or hitherto law abiding citizens; or that each area is endeavoring to enhance its arsenal so as to gain a decisive edge. It does not matter; what matters is that these guns are there, out there. It is the firm belief of many that the quantity of illegal guns in this country makes the 30,000 licensed ones melt into insignificance.

What follows next is conjectural, a reasonable "best guess" hazarded, as gleaned, then extrapolated from the intelligence of the day.

Sometime ago, a concerned citizen, who happened to be a ranking public official, found cause to express strong apprehensions concerning the number of illegal guns in this country. She believed that it could be anywhere around the vicinity of 100,000 such weapons. Many think that this is a solid figure, and might even be on the conservative side. This means that there could be one firearm on average for every adult male in this civilization. However, there is nothing "average" about illegal gun possession. The reality is that they are not spread out evenly across the population, many of whom would never go near such things or thoughts. Where is this going? Where does it lead?

The harsh, chilling reality is this: the believed prodigious amount of guns in Guyana is concentrated in the hands of criminal enterprises, the ultra-security conscious, and the politically strategic. Thus, without a doubt, many of these same guns are housed in deep racial and political waters. Therein festers the trouble, the potential for disaster, and the thrust of this chapter.

Now that the issue of quantity and likely ownership of illegal guns has been broached, a stark, distressing conclusion becomes unavoidable.

It is that these guns are currently underground, and kept in readiness for pointing and firing at each other in racial and political conflict, when (when not if) the time and circumstances so demand. No political leader from any quarter can deny this circumstance without incinerating the truth. Then again, in this country political leaders are not overly concerned with the rudiments of truth or principle. In some respects, these guns are reminiscent of the stalemate at the Somme and Verdun during World War I: there they were silent for long stretches of time, but both Englishmen and Germans knew that they were present and always aimed at one another. History did reveal how destructive in life and limb those close quarter encounters proved to be. It is the same story here in Guyana in 2013, except that the guns in the tens of thousands (perhaps a hundred thousand) are all temporarily out-of-sight and under the radar of detection. The safety mechanism is in the "on" position, but for the time being only.

Guns: From Quantity to Quality

It is appropriate to move from possible quantity and ownership of guns to a closer look at the next discomforting question, which is: What kinds of guns are present, compliments of the shadowy world of arms smuggling and gunrunning? What floats up on the screen of discovery, and the never ending episodes of crimes?

It would be constructive to eliminate what is NOT part of the illegal domestic arsenals. There are no old fashioned revolvers; no single-shot, manual relics; no pellet guns and air guns. No, there are none of these. As attested by sporadic seizures and crime forensics, the weapons of choice are high powered, new model, state-of-the-art creations. They are automatic, rapid fire, life shattering instruments with such piercing names as Glock, Sig & Sauer, Uzi, and AK-47. There are sophisticated handguns and machineguns galore. And they are undeniably present in a society fractured along racial lines. The mind calcifies, the gut liquefies, such is the potential for madness, given these tools and resources in hand.

While no one knows for sure where they are concealed, there is enough awareness-solid, incontestable awareness-as to how they get here, and how to get some of them.

There is the awareness of wide, porous borders on almost every cardinal point; of lax and thin law enforcement; of corrupt and cooperative law enforcement; and of busy trading routes, a few known, but most secret. Recent events have provided solid evidence of secret illegal movements involving a dizzying array of species across the national borders in both directions. There has been-and continues to be-movement of desperate people, even more desperate fugitives, vehicles, aircraft, narcotics, gold, and unlimited contraband in a steady flow. There are armed networks dedicated to these schemes and lucrative businesses. There is official involvement on several fronts and from the usual quarters. Because of these known conditions on the ground, there is the high probability of an endless stream of guns snaking its way into the land. An endless stream characterized by bulk shipments and the latest in firepower sophistication. The primary reasons for these shipments might very well be crime and business; or the business of crime. But somewhere in the calculations and objectives, there also can be political resistance, political defense, and political hostilities, in effect the same thing said differently. And however this is viewed, it means preparation for racial confrontation, and armed racial conflict.

The legitimate concerns over where all of this leads is further compounded by ominous, persistent reports of large arms caches in certain communities. These are communities long racially homogenous, and on one side of the political chasm or the other. Their political allegiance is determinedly racial, and fanatically, immovably so. Both believers and doubters should have no issues in figuring out what this means for country and peoples.

Many will not wish to hear this, or to contemplate such unnerving scenarios; they will prefer to bury their heads in the mud in pretended ignorance, and hope for the best. It does not help.

Guns: Smoking then Disappearing

There are some other things that many in this society do not know; or prefer not to know. A cooperating government ensures that they remain in the darkness of their ways.

What is the story with the remaining missing AK-47s removed from the GDF armory? Who took them and for what reasons? Who were they given to? Where are they now? Given that a couple of police ranks were not so long ago caught red-handed looking the other way for a price when they stumbled upon an illegally owned submachine gun in private hands, have others looked the other way too if and when near the missing army automatics?

Sticking with the army, there was an explosion and loss of life at Camp Groomes a decade ago. What is the real story for that explosion? What did the explosion provide cover for? What has been covered up from public view? It is mighty peculiar that a usually garrulous government has been unusually reticent in sharing information on this particular incident. Perhaps, it does not desire to induce panic. Perhaps the racial political mileage to be gained is outweighed by the secrets concealed ....

Last, move over to the public marketplace. It is not quite the open-air gun show extravaganzas like the American ones in the Deep South, as shown on TV. The Guyana gun marts are more clandestine; a sort of stealth operation. But they do exist. One can visit certain venues and purchase an illegal firearm. There is some variety, and they are surprisingly inexpensive and affordable. One makes a choice, leaves a trifle heavier in the stride, and with the beginning of a swagger in comportment. Yes, it is this easy. For a higher price, the sellers offer supposedly "clean" weapons. Meaning that these have not been involved in the commission of a crime; the ballistics are pure. The dilemma for the buyer is this: How can that be proved? Regardless, the key is the ease of availability of firearms in the middle of routine, everyday commercial bustle. It is disturbing.

This is the story-the concealed, though sometimes known truth-concerning the stockpiles of illegal guns in this country. They hold the potential for dire peril, cataclysmic in proportion, reach, and sweep. It is racial in outlook and national in implications.

The Men Behind the Guns –Who are They?

So much for the presence of vast quantities of guns. What about the men behind the guns? Who are they? What are they called? What is their thinking? Who do they work for? Who is the bulk of their victims? How far will they go?

While this could be divided into the criminal, political, and commercial, it must be stated right from the start that there is significant concentricity-sometimes inseparably so-in these streams of activity. The prime movers behind the scenes could be wearing more than one hat, sometimes all three. This is how the story goes.

PHANTOMS AND PHANTOM SQUADS FIRST

The men behind the guns have been called different names by opposing people who have clashing agendas. A Prime Minister called them "criminal gangs" in the early, formative days; a claim was made by Black Guyanese for "freedom fighters" and "resistance fighters;" and Indians and the PPP took a resolute stand on behalf of "crime-fighters." Into this hallowed pantheon of gory heroes, martyrs, serial killers, stone killers, child killers, desperadoes, deportees, escapees, and aggressors and defenders stepped a memorable figure with an even more memorable phrase. The phrase now indelibly enshrined in infamy or glory-contingent upon perspective-is "phantom squad." The author of the phrase was none other than chief medicine man, chief ruling party spokesman, government salesman-in-chief, Dr. Roger Luncheon. But the local Dr. Kildare, characteristically cute and clever with his verbal anesthetics only identified part of the matter.

This unrepentant, sometimes majestic obfuscator, spoke in the singular –of "a phantom squad." The heart of the matter is that there are a number of these so-called phantom squads, and no one knows for sure the precise count. In fact, it might be appropriate to say that some of these squads are not strictly phantomlike anymore, but known and identifiable. Both major parties have one (or more), which can be summoned to do dirty political work. Not surprisingly, some of the surgical operations usually result in victims of a particular racial stripe among the fallen.

Moreover, this same oracle of official truth was careful to leave the small matters of association, ownership, and sponsorship of his self-described phantom squad unaddressed and dangling. This was deliberate. The revelations from succeeding years have shown the answers to those matters to be close to the political roost –his own. Today, the once surging clamor about crime-fighters and defenders of the realm has been quietly abandoned;

crime-fighters it must be said who had a lengthy period of notoriety, and engaged in a range of nefarious activities that saw a lot of people shot down, most of whom were Black.

Separately, criminal groups have their own squads, businesspeople have their hit men, and the police have their executioners.

Most Guyanese who care believe certain infallible truths: that multiple phantom squads exist; they will do any kind of killing; and they are temporarily dormant, as dictated by circumstances, some of which are political. They constitute a robust reserve force yoked to racial, political-and adversarial-alliances. They are mercenaries who work for reward, and loyalists who work for the current and later rewards of spoils on the ground. And then there are those not overly loyal racially. In other words, they will kill their own for a price. In aggregate, this represents a large pool-segments of which are not known-of executioners and foot soldiers all armed to the teeth and available for business interests or political upheaval or racial cleavage; they have been so used before in each respect.

This is what the bottom line adds up to and leads: there are countless sophisticated guns in Guyana in determined hands; those hands and guns have already reaped a savage harvest of racial blood and racial flesh. Those hands are ready to work with those guns. Again. Both guns and hands stand ready and available to unleash more of the same cyclonic racial blast experienced in the recent past in the future. The difference promises to be of a heavier uncontrolled intensity, and for a more protracted period of time.

Extremists Again: Myth or more ....?

For its part, the PPP has not been on the defensive where the killings are concerned. Though clearly identified with phantoms and phantom enforcers who did political protection work, which resulted in many racial murders, it has moved quickly to slam the door shut on strong beliefs about racial discontent, strife, and division. The party will have none of such dirty talk. It is counterproductive and unhealthy for stretched Indian nerves. Thus, its leaders, opinion shapers, thought police, and propaganda machinery busy themselves with the farce of "extremists" bulldozing their way forward to create racial fissures and disunity in society.

Almost by definition, extremists should be a minority, an uncontrollable, hostile minority, but a minority nonetheless. This is comforting to those Indian listeners who will grasp at any straw; and works to the added purpose of diluting Black anger, solidarity, and movement. It seeks industriously to dilute cohesion and agitation with the recognition of "only a few." So there, no problem! Nothing could be more spurious and further from the reality.

Despite the happy talk-perhaps because of it-thinking people are not fooled. Not Indians, and certainly not Black Guyanese. For example, no Guyanese in his or her right senses believes that 'Fineman' Rawlins was responsible for ALL the killings allocated to him. Or that some of the arson attacks on government buildings can be sourced solely to this omnipotent handful of "extremists." Meaning Black opposition extremists. Or that there is only one group of such "extremists" which recalls the specter of multiple phantom squads. Or that these so-called extremists are stashed away in only opposition enclaves.

With this in mind, and moving farther afield, the failure to pinpoint a source-or sources-for the Linden killings turns responsibility on its head. If not the police, then who? Are the opposition extremists now murdering their own? Perhaps, the objective was to trigger limited racial strife; to teach a lesson through hardline responses; or to provide graphic persuasive footage for hesitant and absentee voters. So the question is tabled: who are the extremists here?

At this point, a simple fact ought to be recognized: It is that a forest fire begins with a flicker, a spark; it then rages uncontrollably. Extremists are the human equivalent of that spark; they can rally mobs out of nowhere, which have neither origin nor structure nor set procedure. These mobs can flow from nothing; and are energized by rumors, speculations, misunderstandings, new opportunities, and old resentments. This is fertile ground for extremists, whether concocted or genuine, be they few or many, In Guyana, the soil is ripe; it is rich; it waits; it beckons. Hence, the PPP myth of a few extremists could very well blow up in its face for they have guns, visions, objectives, and a wall of simmering people behind them.

Finally, there are only two questions left: What is the thinking of the men-the real big, "nonpolitical" men-behind the profusion of guns? How far will they go to maintain their own established presence and a friendly, supportive status quo?

The Local Faces of Foreign Interests

First, it must be made clear, that to them (foreign interests) this is about business, pure and simple. Despite the nastiness of violence and blood and death, it is nothing more than keeping the rackets running smoothly and uninterruptedly. This is how uncomplicated things are. Second, wrap the mind around these two points: Guyana does not cultivate narcotics crops, be they leaves and flowers that culminate in the production of cocaine, heroin, opium, or whatever sells riotously. It has no processing laboratories buried deep in the wilds of the hinterlands. Product for the trade comes from else-where —meaning overseas. Second, the vast oceans of currency that circulates in this country and serves as grotesque caricatures of personal elevation and national development do not originate with the Bank of Guyana, or from the fruits of honest legitimate labor. No folks! It comes from the great beyond, as in the blue yonder to the north; and it comes in dollars not pesos or bolivars.

Since the underlying product and the derivative proceeds are both from other lands, this points to foreign controllers and masters, who are the original distributors and directors of both merchandise and money. These are serious men, and they are in heaven. Unfortunately for residents of this land, their heaven is a nightmarish problem for local society. How so?

Because Guyana incorporates the most perfect convergence of circum-stances possible. With its porous colander-like borders, its compromised institutions (police, Customs, Prisons, courts, airport for starters), its polit-ical facilitators, its poverty, and its everything-is-for-sale reality, this coun-try is Nirvana for the men blocked from shipping directly to destination markets, and banking the proceeds openly. Guyana makes both activities possible, and seamlessly, too. It is the place to setup shop using willing local proxies operating under a plethora of fronts in a cash intensive society. It does not get any better than this.

The foreign suppliers and strategists have been hugely successful. Here is the problem for Guyanese: They will not be moved. They will fight. They will go to war, or foster war if they feel threatened and do not get their way. It is no exaggeration to say that this includes civil war. The lan-guage of superpowers and diplomats is apropos. Guyana has become a vital transit point like the Suez Canal and the Strait of Hormuz. It is now noto-rious for both transshipment activities outward, and as a pipeline through which dirty money is funneled inward. It is too incomparably valuable an asset, which must be prevented from slipping out of grasp and control. At all costs and by any means necessary. Usually this means appalling and unimaginable violence. Remember Bogota and Medellin in Columbia. Think Guadalajara and Juarez in Mexico now. Yes, it is time to flinch and cringe, for this is the level of violence promised. And if push comes to shove, no one here can prevent matters from coming to this sorry pass.

Look around and listen: No one bothers anymore to deny the political-narcotic-commercial complex and nexus. Especially the principals. Other than the occasional feeble protestations, there is the solidity of blank silence. Let the focus linger on the politicians. This means funding through large loads of currency for political interference and protection; this has been seen and is known. This means welcome and acceptance in the highest circles for local kingpins. They deliver the goodies. This could be suitcases of money for election purposes, and to make the routine obstructions of the regular day go away. But the ties are not limited to cash only: there were the guns and phantom force made available a few short years ago. Their job was straightforward —maintain the political status quo, which translated to a mini race conflict.

In view of all of this, the ruling party knows that its bread is thickly buttered on every side. Therefore, it must earn its keep, and justify its presence and longevity by keeping the coast clear and hospitable. Having enjoyed the fruits of its treacherous labors, there is no desire to derail the rich gravy train by developing a sudden attack of conscience and principle.

Just as importantly, the PPP knows that it is a small matter for the overseas bosses to switch their invisible backing, financial muscle, and accumulated firepower to the other side. That would be the dreaded, hated PNC. All it would take is an instructive word and a clearing nod to the local apparatus. As stated before, it is only business and protecting the pipelines on the ground. And the first order of business is continuity. Should difficulty arise about working together, unreliability, or newfound patriotism, then it would be the time to switch partners and alter irreversibly the status quo of the last two decades. There is a sufficiency of guns, money and other resources, and manpower to make such a change happen. Locals will cooperate in the interests of their own survival; if they do not, there are other hungry groups longing for a chance to sell themselves, to be purchased, and to replace the others.

Now if anyone shouted "civil war" that might be a tad premature, somewhat hasty. But it cannot be ruled out. In the same breath, it must be said that the foundations for racial strife and conflagration are already in place. They will be exploited and leveraged, if the necessary results are produced. All options would be on the table. It would come down to a matter of which approach best fits the bill, gets rid of obstacles, and get business back on track and moving. Collateral damage, loss of life and property are not worthy considerations to the foreigners; they will send in their own shooters at times, and are not in the caring and compassion business. Just ask the surviving families of the man tortured and killed in Herstelling in the 1980s, and then exhumed and decapitated a year later at the Le Repentir cemetery; and more recently the chilling 'Cold Beer' execution at the GMRC. In sum, the foreigners can do what they want, when they want, and to whom they want. This is the nitty-gritty of where this country finds itself today, thanks to those who opened this Pandora's Box. It is stark, it is insurmountable.

Over five years ago, it was opined that "control of this country has passed." It is worse now, more entrenched, more irremediable. It is a sorry thought, a sorrier state.

This chapter commenced with the proliferation of guns. Then, it strapped those guns to the body politic and outlined the racial possibilities. Next, it pointed to the willingness of both major parties to bring out the big guns ('long guns'" is the favored local descriptive) and unleash them in deadly racial fusillades. Further, there was comment on sophisticated arsenals assembled for later developments. Even further, there was the recognition of shadowy phantom forces present to put boots on the ground and warheads where needed. Last there was movement away from the fateful domestic crossroads of guns, politics and race, and the introduction of the foreign factor.

This was the new composite face of narcotics and money laundering, the ruthless objectivity of the narcotics business powers, and the devastating implications for Guyana and Guyanese of all races. The common denominator, the irrepressible enabler is guns. It is the here and now, and life and death; it could very well be the final political and racial solution. With the horrifying presence of so many guns and formidable characters, what are some of the things that have served as momentary restraining forces? What are the myths propagated and the tactics employed to dilute and diminish abiding insecurities?

CHAPTER XI

Myths and Realities: Paternalism, Unity, Democracy, Hate and Escape Valves

"We do not want freedom fed to us in teaspoons over the next 150 years."
-Martin Luther King

Those words of Dr. King stir. They have an ominous ring, even coming from the apostle of nonviolence. They point to the teaspoons sloshed and slicked with deceptive syrupy words, the galling specks of charity, and a treacherous brotherhood. They are not enough, they are wasted. They are damned for the state to which they reduce the recipients.

Paternalism: The Happy Contented Negro

The Black segment of the populace is tired and ashamed of the dribs and drabs doled out to their communities. They resent mightily the paternalism, the dependency. But at every opportunity that presents itself, the PPP and its leading spokespersons will rush forward to recite how much money and how much assistance it has directed to non-Indian communities; there are all these statistics, roundly ignored and condemned; and there is always the reference and comparison to the record of the PNC times. Rightly or wrongly, it is water on a duck's back, as no one cares, and all of this means nothing.

In addition, there is a school of thought within the party's hierarchy, which permeates to the wider rank and file level. It is this: How much more do these people want? What else are they going to ask for, nay demand? What is it going to take to satisfy them? There is the strong belief in PPP circles that its conduct with regard to the Black community borders on the irreproachable. What it refuses to understand-indeed, to discern and accept-is that the skimpy occasional benevolence is not enough. Much more is required than the paltry handouts and the occasional monetary pats on the back to still the agitation and resistance in the street and soul. It is the nuanced approach that focuses on a prolonged dedicated search for balance along a broad front and on an extensive menu of matters. It is, on the one hand, a balance that consists of the monetary, the developmental, and the remedial, which is palpable in content; and the intangible of reaching in emotional and psychological compatibility, on the other.

But the PPP, as party and government will have none of this; it is content with deliberate and benign neglect. It wants all for itself and its favored few. It will not be moved to reach out and share equitably and consistently in genuine partnership; it is cheaper to put out fires and buy off selfish Black leaders, and venal Black collaborators. There is no identification with the despair of the struggling; there is no understanding for those who believe with a passion that they are being discriminated against; and there is little recognition of the scorn that results from the piecemeal, stopgap approaches employed; or that the Band-Aids last for only a short period of time, before they lose adhesion and effect.

Along these lines, there was this leader who fancied himself a domestic John Wayne on a white charger. He would gallop hither and thither to this or that conflict situation, and bring order to the restless natives. This was the governing idea behind winning hearts and opening minds in the Black communities; this was the substitute for concerted action and authentic, long lasting partnering; and this was the fast moving solution to the bleak everyday realities of want and hunger, and of anger and despair.

Hence, the dividing and ruling, the sowing of distrust and fear, and stoking of old antagonisms all help to keep the pendulum of power frozen in its fateful advantageous PPP swing. It must not go back to the Black side. According to the self-perpetuating mythology in the minds of the PPP brass, this means that the Black race should resign itself to surrender to a democracy of eternal dominance, and an uninterrupted continuum of dependency. This has to be a paradise of fools; or a political asylum infested with lunatics. Whichever one it happens to be, it will blow up in the face of this nation with staggering consequences in a society totally lacking in unity.

The Pretense to Unity –Empty Intentions, Emptier Actions

If deceptive political rhetoric was crude oil, this country would be like Saudi Arabia –floating on an endless ocean of it. Such is the richness of the local rhetorical reservoir, and never more so than when the issue is about unity. PNC attitudes and conduct rose to the level of a virtual felony, and the PPP's behavior in this regard amounts to an ongoing capital offense. Nobody believes any of the speciousness that makes the rounds anymore; all grimace knowingly. This is how unconvincing any such unguent has become. Thus public pronouncements from on high (read the president) about "unity" and standing for "all Guyanese" are received as so much recycled hogwash. They are interpreted, quite accurately, as careful public relations exercises, a sop to political correctness, and a painstaking dedica-tion to making the right utterances for the record and history. This "going through the motions" serves no purpose, other than to mock an already jaded citizenry.

Nobody is fooled –not Indians, not Black people, not anybody. Yet the PPP and its addled brain trust persists with this low-level Mexican standoff that deteriorates into real fires, real bullets, and real dead bodies on occasions.

When examined against reality, there is nothing. Nothing was intended; nothing is shared. Unity will not be achieved by a politician making a speech, and then resting in mesmerized self-satisfaction to the soft rustle of his words. There are things that have to be done: hard decisions to be made, stubborn supporters to be persuaded, and hostile foes to be won over. It does not come overnight, it is trial and error, it might even be futile; and it is definitely thankless. But deeds have to follow the words and the embedded vision; else there is nothing. Unless the calls for unity were not intended to mean anything right from the beginning. Given that people and community are pitilessly squeezed, that their pain and suffering evoke little interest, and that their stagnation grows inexorably, then it has to be concluded that twaddle about "unity" is filling up space and the ultimate in rank cheap deception. Then there is this business of democracy, and its significance in Guyana, and for Black Guyanese.

Democracy: Rewarding to Winners, Punishing to Losers

In the textbooks, and as a political principle, it is noble and enlightening, and to which every superlative can be attached, when compared to other forms of representation. As a reality, it can be heaven for the victors and purgatory for the losers. In mature, sophisticated societies, there is some give-and-take, partial lifting up of losers in their long moment of descent, and ongoing majority interest in the lot of minorities. It takes time. More importantly, it takes the right men and women, armed with the right intentions, and infused with a powerful will –a will that will not be denied.

With the exception of the hagiographers and clever revisionists, most will agree that the peoples of Guyana have suffered terribly from the presence of the wrong men and women. Men and women who exhibited the worst of intentions, and were (are) bereft of the will to do what is right and commit themselves to whatever it takes to make this a harmonious society. The result is that this fragile philosophy called democracy holds local society with all the strength of a slender thread. It is a thread that does not-and cannot-bind. It means little in the realm of the loser, it produces mucus and spittle; for those on the margins, it is as welcome as a snake under the pillow; or in the shoe. It is feared, suspected, and reviled by those who come out second. There is nothing for them, other than the daily reminders of their misery.

In Guyana, what passes for democratic leadership is fingernail strong, skin deep, and race stained. It is a wonderful rewarding life for the overseers and horsemen in the saddle; it is, however, a harrowing existence for the horses first overburdened, then repeatedly abused, and last thoughtlessly goaded to greater effort and submission. Now that it is in power, the PPP is content to pontificate about democracy that is punitive, and freedoms that mean nothing to losers.

None identifies more with the appalling conditions, the stultifying dreariness, and increasing weariness of those horses than the Black man in Guyana. To be sure, there are destitute Indians, indigenous peoples, and others almost similarly yoked and punished. But none descends to the bitter depths experienced by Black communities and Black people. For them, this is not academic wrangling, but of simple hunger. For them, there is none of the light of conceptual purity, only the grey bleakness of opportunity removed and aspirations restricted. And for the Black Guyanese, there is no Churchillian acceptance as the best form of government, rather there is only the blight of a visionless future. For the Black man, democracy, such as it exists, is yoke and prison. It is also gutting and demoralizing. And through all of this injury and indignity, he is expected to grin and be of good cheer. Oh, and by the way, it was once postured that the Black discontented are only a small number.

From Narrow Inconsequential
Extremists to Broad Frightening Hate

The PPP people say it is the agitation of a handful of "extremists;" the work of a vocal, nefarious minority. This is what, at convenient times, the top guys and propaganda machinery, have churned out to feed the nation, especially anxious Indians. It is an absurdity, a lie, an absolute falsehood. These same leaders and their very skilled supporting cast tell the nation in the next breath that these extremists are part of a determined, sinister opposition phalanx. This is called straddling the line, through ignoring reality, and perpetuating a larger lie. What the ruling party does not reveal to the nation is that some of those same racial "extremists" are part of its own fold, and very prominent in its flock, where the race issue is concerned; the *modus operandi* is sowing dissension and fear among its followers. In the next instance, the party lobbies very actively to brainwash Guyanese-none more so than Indians-that the Black peril is known and isolated; that it is under control and of little significance. It is soothing.

Some time ago, the nation heard repeatedly shrill utterances about a tiny band of "extremists" at large operating under the cover of darkness. They were these mysterious figures involved in even more mysterious arsons and suspicious incidents deliberately shrouded in official secrecy. Extremists hinted as belonging to the main opposition PNC; and who attack the Indian power structure, and readying to pulverize private Indian targets. So, according to PPP mythology, the race issue is minimal, almost nonexistent, and there is no live racial tripwire. This is good for public relations, and bestows upon the party the mantle of unifying force where race relations are concerned. It first dilutes, then dismisses tensions surrounding widespread Black anger and solidarity. The myth of the "Happy Contented Negro" is resurrected. But that was then; it is no longer convenient now.

Recall the president at Babu John recognizing the broad, troubling aspects of political life in Guyana, when he spoke of "hate" and "haters." Through his flowing excoriation, and pointed message, the president inadvertently signaled his recognition of the roots of the issue. And it is not limited to the myth and speciousness of a tiny handful of "extremists." The words "hate and "haters" are very strong, cover wide areas, and encircle a whole lot of either angry-or fearful-people. Those words were well-chosen and well-placed; few words are as ominous, and disturbing in Guyana's political context; the president knew what he was saying, and where he was going. All in all, they are on-the-money and spell serious trouble for this country.

If all of this is so, and since this country has some obvious vulnerabilities, what has stayed the hand of the discontented, potential rebels, and extremists? What has temporarily diluted the deep resentments and even deeper anger that glow incandescently? Since the racial temperature is seen to be at such a combustible level, how is it that there have not been more explosions? A host of reasons surfaces immediately in answer to these prickly questions; a few are now offered and discussed. They are mainly money centric, and range from foreign factors to domestic norms. A look is taken at the local vulnerabilities first, before moving on to reconfigured foreign interests, and last to the balms of local release valves.

Known Vulnerabilities

The business and administration of this society is still heavily concentrated, in spite of the ongoing geographical diversification of commerce and some government services. Arguably, its heart, oxygen supply, and mind remain housed in tiny, congested Georgetown, which makes it extremely easy to identify pressure points and choke points. The main political players know them; they have lived there before.

These pressure points, vulnerabilities might be more apropos, are not many. Think key intersections, courts, and jails. Individually and as part of a continuum, there is susceptibility to prolonged siege and overcrowding. There are only so many bodies that can be absorbed at street level, then processed and accommodated in official holding areas. Capacity is severely limited, and all would come to a standstill, including vital commerce, especially commerce. AND ALL WITHOUT LIFTING A SINGLE THREATENING HAND, WITHOUT UTTERING A SINGLE HOSTILE WORD, OR WITHOUT RAISING ONE ANGRY VOICE. Some should recall the Greensboro Four and 1960. Those who might lack memory or the familiarity of history can watch and see though.

Guyana watched when Agricola froze the East Bank Demerara and across the river; Guyanese looked on as Linden virtually shut down a large section of the interior. Both were violent, and both were eye opening, when neither should have been. For such is the vulnerability of this society, that when a wrist is bent, other parts of the body grind to a halt. The PPP and the PNC both know this, too. Both also know in their own way that the capital city is the head: If it is surrounded and squeezed for too long, it experiences a rush of ailments – political hypertension; institutional seizures; commercial paralysis; social dizziness; and racial fibrillation. In layman's terms, Georgetown would be laid out flat. AND THE REST OF LOCAL SOCIETY WITH IT. Guyanese leaders need no tutoring from anyone on the effects of nonviolent resistance; the pages of history relay well the sagas of noble sacred struggle in East and West.

But no one is ready just yet to suffocate the street, overwhelm the courts, and overcrowd the jail. Why? It starts with the desire of the collective heart, and vision of the collective mind; and it continues with hard, unbearable sacrifice to make destiny happen, to make it beckon. There is little by way of mental preparedness to take that first step, that long punishing crawl. And, in contrast, there is much in the physical presence of release valves, which brings the relief of temporary amnesia and escape at the individual level.

Two Momentary Escape Valves

First, there is the huge sucking vacuum of migration. Whether legal or illegal, short-term or long-term, migration in all its sundry elements offers a sliver of hope to those on the way, and a connecting thread to those left behind. There is anticipation of relief from everyday woes through remittances, and hopes of escape through flight generated by the prospect of following later. Not surprisingly, the dismay and rage over poverty, want, and political criminality is tranquilized by the arrival of cash, barrel, or the call to go. The waiting refuse to be overly exercised, their eyes are on a bigger prize –leaving. In some senses, Guyana is a holding pen for many, and the searing concerns of the day and circumstances, inclusive of racial injury and indignity, are eased by the promises of "getting out" or "getting something."

Both Black and Indian Guyanese are always on the lookout for that call and movement to the "outside." But, it is widely accepted that Indians will go the extra mile (and many extra dollars) to get away, which says volumes about the PPP itself. They rush desperately, through visa or backtrack, for betterment elsewhere, and to leave behind the poverty, fears, and tensions. If this is the mindset of the poor-and other-Indians, then it goes without saying that the outlook of the Black Guyanese is much more harrowing, and distinctly more infuriating. The constant traffic, however, of both races redirect their attention and priorities away from the ills of the times; it helps to defuse the pressures building in society.

Second, the parallel or underground economy provides another recognizable release valve. These are the massive, hugely lucrative businesses of narcotics shipments and money laundering; AND the political hub to which these businesses are attached, and around which they revolve. In the first instance, there is a lot of work-dirty work-to be done, which demands labor. There is demand for transporting, for smuggling, for killing, for guarding, and any other duties assigned, none of which honest folks would consider aboveboard. Most of the dirty work has been farmed out to Black underlings, who revel in their role as "gangstas." The pay is not minimum wage, as money is not a problem. This kind of employment and purchasing power affords immersion in conspicuous consumption through wine, women, song, dance, wheels, and threads to the point of over-satiation. Times are good and there is money in Black pockets and some Black homes, compliments of an Indian dominated trade. It assists in harnessing energies and keeping things cool.

In the second instance, there is the urgent need to do something with all the foreign proceeds from dirty business that gathers around idly. This "doing something' has to pass muster, must appear to be clean. Hence the spectrum of fronts and covers, as embodied in the presence of construction and buildings, bars and stores, dredging and driving (cab service), to name a few in an endless variety of nebulous, illegitimate activities. The point is that there is hustling frenzy and turnover for materials required, and there are bodies at work. The latter would include carpenters, masons, laborers, clerks, salespeople, and so on and so forth. The government calls this progress and development, with a cartoonlike expression and total unconcern. Citizens limit themselves to the discernment of bad business and criminal activity. Regardless, there are these undeniable facts: people are employed, money changes hands, food is on the table, bills are paid, and some joy is spread. As can easily be seen, lots of things are made possible by the presence and scope of the underground economy. It contributes to ignoring the troubles of the day, forgetting the plight of one's suffering kinsmen, and doing concrete work while the sun is shining.

Some knowledgeable people have ventured that the underground economy in Guyana could be anywhere from forty to sixty percent of the total national economy. Even if it is twenty-five percent, which nobody believes for a minute, it would be a staggering number. Whatever the number, the last word is this: individuals are occupied, engaged, and rewarded at the lower rungs. Many are in private practice, they have counterparts in officialdom. Together this serves to dissipate some of the energy, discontent, and anger. Only some, but it provides the relief of escape valves from the underlying racial stresses and fears. It should be remembered that for every one individual pacified by migration, or who benefits from involvement in dirty business, there are several hundred left out in the cold. They are hungry, they are tired, and they are simmering. They live in anger and distrust; and with hate. The president himself said so, didn't he?

CHAPTER XII

WHITHER LOCAL SOCIETY ...

"O ye immortal gods, where on earth are we?
In what city are we living? What
constitution is ours?"
-Cicero

Guyana languishes in restless torment. Part of it seethes, another tenses. There is watchfulness, empty courtesy, stony silence, vacant distance, cool dismissal, constant abrasiveness. Amidst the occasional deep genuine friendships, and the rare implacably honest discussions and evaluations, this is local society in the core of its divided soul. It is more than the haves and the have-nots; more than who robs and who is violated. It is about who is fit to rule, and who should not be ruled. Now for the questions: What lies in store for this society? Where will the miseries of division, racial tension, discontent, and anger lead? In what manner will the aggregated frustrations of the endless day and the tortured soul culminate? What price is there to be paid for the purposeful failure to heed national frailties, and not to seek genuine, lasting solutions? Given the incarceration of the past and the stranglehold of the present, what is the promise of the future? What can be the promise of the future? Is there one?

Tomorrow: A Path to Self-Destruction

The present and future-whether near or further away-point toward deepening cleavage and a path leading to self-destruction. This society and its peoples cannot continue as it stands; it lacks the sacred tradition, indefinable pride, and the imperishable ideals to bind it together. Indeed, it is a small miracle that it has held for so long, given how tenuous this has been. The cleavage has already been intolerably distressing: it suffocates, it imprisons. Inexorably.

On occasion, there has been release through violent haphazard squalls; the energy and poisons were all present and visible. And felt too. But so far, and for the time being, these racial explosions have lacked bulk, potency, and direction. They are like those seasonal hurricanes that threaten: They swirl and rage, aim for land, lose intensity and force, follow a different track, and fizzle out weakly over uncontested space. False alarms, or bullets dodged, are how these are described. There is a telling difference between nature and man though: whereas nature retreats and dissipates, man remembers and regroups, his agitations and turbulences are layered and longer lasting. Man remembers; he waits and plans.

Has this not been the case for concerned, apprehensive citizens in Guyana? Is this not what they live with like vulnerable riverside communities standing defenselessly in the path of hurricanes? Except that the menacing domestic disaster-in-waiting is manmade and man-powered? And just like those super storms that can develop out of nowhere, there will be one that scythes a path of destruction over one and all here. Monsters such as these know neither friend nor enemy, rich or poor, guilty or innocent. It is just the way they are; they take everything out when they happen.

By way of a quick digression, the title of this book involves a volcano, which image has been interspersed intermittently across the pages. The analogy of hurricanes from the preceding paragraph illuminates the local condition in a different way. Either one should register powerfully with Guyanese. The warning is the same: great danger lurks. Perhaps preparations are in order; remedial actions to be pondered and embraced. There has long been a belief amongst Guyanese that this nation is lucky. They look around the Caribbean and see and hear of the terrible devastation wreaked by forces of nature, including not infrequent hurricanes and the occasional volcano. There is collective gratitude for being spared the devastation and trauma. When looked at differently, perhaps this nation has not been spared at all, in that its terror and devastation come from the storms within; that is, from the runaway power of a tainted body politic, from the chain lightning of racial exposure, and from the superheated lava that incinerates the national soul. Maybe Guyana is not so lucky when all is considered.

But that is tomorrow. What about today? Where do things stand right now?

Today: The Here and Now

Today Guyanese of all races live with the knowledge of division; it is undeniable. It is just as undeniable that this division widens daily, and grows more sensitive, with each new revelation, new frustration, and new concern. There was the October surprise in 2012 of Agricola; it could have been anyplace else, but it should not have been. An entire corridor-the only one-stalled in helplessness and fear for an interminable period; significant segments of the populace raged and cowered in turn. It was one racial minefield that exploded with sharp suddenness. This time there was no igniting into the feared-chain reaction. Emphasis is placed on this time.

Agricola demonstrated beyond the shadow of a doubt, the volatile explosive nature of discontent, anger, and racial attributes in this country. Agricola is not an aberration; it is not an isolated rogue community. Whether politically instigated or extremist generated-and everyone recognizes that it is more than the combined force of both elements-Agricola happened; and there are other Agricolas that exist elsewhere. Agricola lives in the hearts of the disenchanted, the impoverished, the injured, and the neglected, wherever they might be in Guyana. AND THIS IS NOT ABOUT MALCONTENTS AND OPPORTUNISTS. Those are the outliers; there is a much larger mass simmering and heaving right in the midst.

Let the truth be faced: Agricola was not about one so-called provocative word; or one irresponsible, unthinking ruling politician; or one more fateful killing in a long line of such inexplicable, senseless killings. No, it was much more than all of this combined. It was (as stated publicly previously) a representation of "the incandescence of countless injustices." However well-received, however scorned, however rickety and condemned for being without foundation, it is what is perceived and believed. Perceived and believed. And lived.

Yes, it is the bright burning light of the countless injustices of extra-judicial killings of mainly Black males; the countless injustice of depressed Black communities brought under government jackboot and grounded into the dust; the countless injustices of inequitable distribution of national resources. And all of which is compounded, and made infinitely more intolerable, by the plunder of those same resources by political scoundrels primarily Indian in origin. On and on sound the wails of Black pain, Black anguish, and Black despair. No one listens. No one cares. Yesterday it was Agricola. Where will matters erupt tomorrow? Will the racial volcano erupt in just an Agricola alone? What about Buxton and Linden and Den Amstel and New Amsterdam and Georgetown and all the other places where people simmer in the void of suffering days and fevered sensibilities? Will they frown only, and accept forever? Will they submit into eternity, and to an eternity of the empty?

The short answer is: NO! The long answer is NO! The only answer is NO!

Tomorrow will not be of an Agricola alone: There are large swarms of Guyanese who feel like the people of Agricola, they hate where they are, and they just don't care anymore. Daily, hourly, individually and collectively the emotional embers glare, they spark; they burn; but they do not burn themselves out. Instead, they are rekindled and reenergized by the newest obscenities that mock and dismiss all fears and all concerns. What is there left to lose? How much farther is there to fall? Who cares about consequences, given the unremitting gloom of existing on the knees? Who knows how matters would unfold, and where things could lead?

What Chance Change –People and Leaders

To restate the obvious, the existing political culture that has been cultivated for so long, and which flourishes, must change. For the sake of national survival and continuity, the longstanding respective mentalities of "apaan jaat" and "kith and kin" must give way to a different vision –one that is genuinely unifying, and to which serious political capital is committed to by both sides. **There will be no change**, however. Clearly this is not going to happen anytime soon, or anytime for that matter; the respective racial mindsets are too irreversibly cemented. In this environment, change, movement, issues, inclusivity, and equity are curse words with dirty meanings. Thus, there will be no change in political structure, thinking, or action. That is, no voluntary change for the other side or the other man. None is to be expected, none to be implemented, as none is contemplated.

There is just too much old and new ugliness; instigated memory; undiluted bitterness; fissured history; stored rage; and determined indoctrination. This hobbles first, and then contributes to individual and tribal immovability. There is no new thinking, only political myopia; no crucial propelling issue, save for race and blind, crippling loyalty. This is what Indians and Blacks in Guyana live for, who they are. They know nothing else, aspire to nothing more.

A relative handful did dare to be different though, especially on the Black side.

History reveals that a recognizable bloc of Black Guyanese was associated with the PPP in its formative years, and that others gravitated later towards the promised difference held out by the AFC. Still, these subsections within the Black voting populace have been too few in numbers, and lack the heft of core and mass. On the other hand, Indians have stuck-with very few exceptions-stuck immovably with the PPP; they have been blindly unwavering in loyalty and voting. That is, until the 2011 national elections, when they stayed away in the tens of thousands to register disgust at, and condemnation of, the obscene levels of corruption committed by party people and tacitly condoned by party brass. But it is all they did –stay away. There is the high probability that already they might have experienced a change of heart-or been squeezed by well-paid and well-placed political touts-with the result that they will make a hurried return to the racial fold. So, it is back to the old square one of "same story, different day."

Now, it is true that Indians did engage in this "poll protest." It is also accurate to state that very few, if any, entertained any inkling of a thought whatsoever of "crossing the polling floor" so to speak, and voting for one of the opposition parties. And certainly most recoiled from the very idea of voting for the reconfigured PNC, now repainted in APNU colors. So for all intents and purposes, the racial silos remain intact, impenetrable, and immovable. Clearly, change is not in the offing, or can incubate under these conditions

With respect to the leaders, none has manifested any interest in going beyond the patter of puerile chatter that embraces the specious, the disingenuous, and the occasionally querulous. Perhaps the capability is lacking. This shabby regiment infested with layers of leaders, EXCOs, power groups, gangs of four (or 35), breakaway parties, so-called dangerous men, wild men, and other assorted racial hustlers lack the brains and intestinal sturdiness to offer a different vision, to attempt a new direction, to make a difference. There is only political cowardice.

Think of this: There is so much deep-seated distrust and dislike between dogfighting, race-touting leaders of the PPP and PNC that they cannot sit together, face each other, and hammer out resolutions to highly problematic issues and concerns; or trust native-born mediators. It is now indelibly engraved in top political minds that anybody who is not a PPP man is automatically a PNC man, and vice versa. No local individual or group is trusted enough, principled enough, sufficiently untouched, to intervene and arbitrate; not church, not civil society, not anybody. Thus, the Linden circumstances (standoff or uprising) required a commission manned by foreigners. This speaks for itself, and is embarrassing. Thus, previous elections impasses that culminated in the deterioration of confrontation found local leaders rushing to Castries and elsewhere, for last ditch rescue operations. The point is that the **bitterness and ugliness is so powerful that we need foreigners to hold our hands, pat our heads, cool our tempers, and sit us down in one place.** LIKE UNRULY UNINTELLIGENT CHILDREN! What will be done-what can we do-when widespread convulsions are the order of the day? Clearly, those who lead do not have what it takes, lacks what is desperately needed.

Most of them do not possess what the national circumstances demand; most of them-if not all-are about self-service, self-preservation, and self-aggrandizement. Whether PPP or PNC (AFC, too), there is one cabal after the other of racial opportunists and users. In substance, it is one huge cabal of political wise-guys who exist in racially parochial habitats.

So far, there has been no leader-or party or committee-sufficiently independent enough in thinking, powerful enough in vision, clean enough in character, to embark first, and then doggedly pursue a different pathway; a pathway that identifies the race poison and peril, then moves to confront, and trample upon, this destructive presence.

No leader would dare to do so, for this is the equivalent of political suicide in Guyana. It is self-destructive in and of itself. This is what props up and invigorates the PPP and PNC –they know nothing else. They wish for no other way. So, within party boiler rooms and officers' quarters, it is all hands on deck, stay the course with what has worked, and look out for self and party first. Thus, there has been one response to calls and hope for change of any kind. It is: To hell with change! Change be damned!

If No Change, Then What?

Since change in the existing political culture and mentality, at all levels, will not happen internally, or voluntarily, or as a matter of higher idealism and patriotism, then there is only a single pathway left –that of force. It is a road of incalculable and unimagined peril. It is where change is forced upon the dull and intransigent. It is where rapidly developing circumstances on the ground will compel compromise and mending of ways, even if only some of the way and for part of the time. The specter of spiraling regional, environmental, physical, personal, and infrastructural disruption, if not devastation, will lead the resisting to the water. Linden and Agricola stand as examples of this. It also provided a case study to the rebellious as to where they went wrong before, during, and after their mini revolts. All should learn.

While the so-called Buxton Uprising and Mash Jailbreak killing sprees were both seen as political conflict, if not naked power plays, the Linden Standoff and Agricola Flare-up were closer to the nature of grassroots, community driven revolts. And revolts they were. It might be argued that there was an invisible political presence, the hand of political instigation, or the perversity of political sponsorship. Maybe so. But the Linden and Agricola revolts were momentary manifestations of the bubbling, heaving volcano underfoot and building towards eruption; eruption, not quite full-fledged blowout. These communities are neither pacified nor satisfied; they are only temporarily quiet, and sullenly so. They are many others like them.

The rest of Guyana saw the neighborhood people-almost all Black-rise up and lash out in anger against the believed oppression and injustice that first cornered them, and then squeezed the life out of them. Guyana saw that overflowing spiraling rage in Linden for many a long day, and in Agricola for one long incendiary moment. Linden and Agricola are representative of the deep-seated fires that consume; they are sharp, irrefutable indicators of what the future holds-always housed-for race relations in Guyana. Those who insist on buoying themselves in a comforting pool of unpersuasive denials, and self-inflicted ignorance, only fool themselves. For there are other places just like Linden and Agricola: They too seethe; for there are other brethren in all these places who feel and think the same way. If anything, these others might be even more hostile, as they strain against the thin shackles of civility and towards the internal call of disobedience and resistance, which many believe, is the answer, the way out. All that is required is a spark, an insinuation, a nudge to provoke reaction-violent reaction-just as has been seen recently in the discontented neighborhoods of Linden and Agricola.

Some will hasten to say that this is not the way, **and it is not**. Violence does not mend; it only ruptures further. There is agreement again. For the downtrodden and dismissed, however, it is all they have left; sometimes it is only what they want to know. Rightly or wrongly, many times violence is viewed as the means towards the hoped for horizon beyond, as a necessary sacrifice, a moving evil. It moves stubborn men to move to the nearness of dialogue, and the table of concession. Call it the street justice of compelled inclusivity. It is temporary though, and it is never enough. But this is what looms, and what endangers. It is the raw, naked reality.

This is the spiraling, momentum gathering, out-of-control circum-stances in which long contained militants and extremists come into their own and flourish. They shake off the residual bonds, they have guns, they emerge from the thick, long suspected, long denied shadows. The other side has defenders, aggressors, and guns, too. As said in a previous chapter, there are many guns, and with them come mayhem, death, and destruction. It is the death of a forced, artificial coexistence; the death of political paralysis and vulgarity; the death of a feigned innocence. And it would be the destruction of all that somehow held things together for so long, and what was known. What the new aftermath would represent is unknown ....

This is the situation: surging and chilling, where the first casualties are moderates and sympathizers and the undecided. Their numbers shrink, voices diminish, and presence and influence disappear. Gone are the restraints of civility, godliness, and humanity. This was seen in miniscule in the last decade or so. There is only the release of long bottled fury, of identifying targets, of eliminating enemies, of settling scores, and of leveling the scales. There are many political and racial scores to settle and many enemies existing; or to be made up or discovered along the way. This has been the brutal lessons from the history of other places; the same brutal lessons have been experienced here, but in more haphazard manner and to a considerably lesser degree.

In this snarling, overflowing racial pressure cooker excess and atrocity multiply. They are magnified for more of the retaliatory. Rumors take wing, mutual fear and hate intensify. Communities respond the only way they know: they shelter, they rally around protectors and warriors; they provide aid and solace. For the sympathetic passive, this is their role: cheer silently from the sidelines, provide moral and spiritual succor. Is this not what happened before?

Take the Buxton community. This Black stronghold, along with a nuanced opposition presence, stood behind their "freedom fighters." The Buxton stronghold did not stand alone with this particular frame of mind. It was the same in the Indian community, and the ruling party, which massed behind its parallel squad of 'crime-fighters.' While the blood flowed and the devastation grew, both ruling and opposition parties provided protective cover. Let the battles continue. Thus, the violence mounted, the bodies fell, and the racial rift tautened more painfully.

Remember Agricola; recall the Speaker of the House and "civil war" the next day; realize what the president was saying about "hate" and "haters" at Babu John. Enough said!

While Buxton was the exception, Linden and Agricola manifested a new phenomenon: there was no vital, controlling center. At times, there were no recognized leaders. This could be the wave of the future where there are only disorganized, disorderly mobs bent on inflicting hurt and terror. These are whipped by the surging energy and adrenalin of the moment, the unconscious cohesion of race, and the uncontrolled momentum of the crowd. Local and foreign history has shown that these are times for killing and destroying.

The Past Points to the Promised Future

What went before in Guyana must be considered to be trivial and episodic, as horrifying as that sounds. As violent and deadly, as all these killing sprees and killing fields undoubtedly were, they constitute only a fleeting shadow of what could be ahead. What they did afford and confirm, however, was a quick preview of some of the armaments, tactics, and forces on the ground.

There was the PPP Congress and Buxton and Agricola and Lusignan and Bartica to name the more horrendous incidents. Automatic weapon fire mowed down the elderly, women, and children. These were not robberies *per se*, but massacres pure and simple; and unambiguously so. In other venues, some of these situations would have in the blink of an eye, be condemned and labeled for what they were: hate crimes, or race crimes, or revenge killings. Here, in Guyana, each was only one more jaded occasion in a succession of jarring, numbing moments.

The killers came with heavy guns by road. On occasion, they were versatile and daring enough to travel by sea and launch amphibious assaults; to commit decoy operations to neutralize pursuers; and to melt away undetected to prearranged bivouacs and waiting safe houses. They had camouflage gear, sophisticated equipment, state-of-the–art technology, and embedded logistical support. The last encompassed food, shelter, medicine, and resupply. Informants and suspected collaborators were methodically eliminated. So too were battlefield enemies. This was WAR! Maybe limited war, but still war.

Dependent upon one's racial loyalties and perspectives, there was a veritable pantheon of either heroes and martyrs, or stone-killers and terrorists. On the one side, there were London, Rawlins, and the Mash Five –all felled by the sword. On the other side, Williams, Fraser, and more coppers than the total that fell in all the years prior. Civilian blood darkened the earth, but they are mere statistics –the price of power or the way to power.

The powers-that-be say there is no need for the drag (and exposures) of ID parades, forensics, and inquiry. Fine Man and Short Man were responsible for all the killings. It is best described as adding darkness to darkness, for a decade later the haziness and uncertainty lingers. Leaders tiptoe around-and back-peddle from-the edges of this dark, bloody chapter in local history. The nation is no closer to truth and accountability. It is one more needle in the racial nerve center.

Hence, the nation speculates-all are expert at this-about who was where and did what. And who at the top of the action, from a covering distance, were really responsible for all the dastardly deeds that happened? Who? It could be that these were some of the names and times and circumstances that so unnerved the Speaker of the House in January 2013.

As vital as knowledge of such occurrences would be, they are secondary to the point being developed here. It is this: a handful of men, well-armed, resourceful, and resolute were able to wreak havoc for long periods of time. They excited racial fears and racial tension, as they killed at will, proved elusive, and left no trail. There are more-many more-of these loyalists and mercenaries available, and who had remained outside the radar of detection. Their ranks have grown in the ensuing lull.

Regardless of which side of the divide the executioners can be found, together and simultaneously they represent formidable forces. These are forces that can launch racial offensives, and provoke revenge actions. The guns are present, the objectives are known. It remains for the will to solidify, which is never a remote or farfetched possibility. For the racially desperate, democracy is meaningless. For them, democracy is the equivalent of soldiers earmarked for suicide missions being assured of the availability of superior health facilities and life insurance coverage; or the starving regaled with the expectation that next year's harvest promises to be bountiful. Desperate people have to get their relief now, and in very tangible form. The alternative is to live on the knees, to plead for indulgence, and to grovel for alms.

The signposts are around –they abound. The thick smoke escapes every so often from the volcano. The warnings go unheeded, there is more merry talk, greater complacency, and more determined resistance to perpetuate the racial discontent and enmity. In the midst of all of this, there is enough fear and disgust, even hate to trigger racial convulsions. There is enough discontent and anger. There are enough guns to make most things possible ....

Is there a way out? What is desperately needed ...

It is said by some that the way out of the political and racial impasse starts with the constitution. That is the cart before the horse, as it is men who make constitutions, and men who make them work. This society longs for, needs, requires groups of men and women-or at least one strong group-that are politically unambiguous; who are racially pure emotionally and mentally; and who have genuine intentions centered on people and country. Where to find? How to induce? There has been enough of the speaking from two faces, and through every possible angle of the mouth. Let there be no more of saying one thing publicly, while instigating something completely opposite secretly; of being, for example, one way in Babu John and Annandale, and another in Buxton and Agricola, and still another at the National Park and Providence Stadium. This has failed the nation, failed it miserably. Unless the brutally frank and the unsparingly honest become the order of the day, the days themselves threaten to be anything but orderly.

Second, any group, any individual that separates self from the common-place vulgar must stand for public service of the highest order, and representative of singular patriotism. The former does not exist at the political level; perhaps, never did in Guyana. It is not limited to catering to the whims of the well-connected, well-established few in the stratospheres of power. It is not about selective caring and outreach reserved for scattered communities of one's own kind. Most of all it is not about the now institutionalized dismissal of the despair of those of another color, of those who stand against.

Rather, public service-or more precisely, political public service-through policy, strategy, and practice is about caring for the people; all the people. There is caring by listening intently and hearing the cries of the poor; recognizing the agony of barren depressed communities; and bringing hope to those who languish in dark seas of hopelessness. Genuine, caring leaders feel the pain of their peoples; they understand and identify with their anguish, and their yearning for relief –any kind of relief that is concrete and just as lasting. Genuine leaders seek to lift up through a coruscating corona of sustained interest, compassion, and action. Such leaders take pride and great joy in giving of self through personal self-sacrifice, and exemplary standards. They do not enrich themselves, while the people grow poorer;

154

they spread scarce resources across the board; they inspire ordinary, every-day people by making a difference in their lives, through offering something to grasp, something to embrace. They are the rising tide that lifts all boats; there are no losers, no enemies.

Third, these individuals must have a strong and abiding distaste-if not hatred-for corruption, whether at the hands of a lowly clerk, or the skull-duggery of a mighty chief. They must be imbued with the reformist zeal and ethical cleanliness of a Lycurgus; they must be ready to turn down a dirty dollar, and turn in a dirtier rogue. The orgies of thievery have to stop, must stop; they divide. If the clean hands are available, and a clean environment is adhered to, then there might be some semblance of hope for this place; only then will the emaciated racial underdog believe. To be clear –some stirrings of hope, not necessarily hope itself.

Are there such Guyanese men and women around, whose first and second friends are patriotism and public service respectively? The answer is yes. That is the good news. The bad news is that it is a tiny handful. Further, the handful so constructed is not inclined to step forward and join the struggle to make this homeland a better place. They are rightfully afraid of being used for nefarious purposes, and shrink from the prospect of contamination through association. These would be individuals who have prospered legitimately, most likely outside of Guyana; individuals who seek no favor from anyone, who take no money, especially the dirty kind; who owe no one; who need no prestige jobs, or status symbols such as opu-lent homes in reserved areas off limits to the regular citizen. They do not need or seek out any such appurtenances and the compromises they inflict on character. In short, they will accept only what is legitimately due and earned; and they care not for anyone's blessing or approval. There is a price attached to resistance and involvement, however. It is best captured by Robespierre when he said: *"Know that any man who will rise to defend public right and public morals would be overwhelmed with outrage and proscribed by the knaves."* Sounds like Guyana, does it not?

Next, any group that seeks to hold itself out as a possible answer must, of necessity, exhibit certain criteria: It must be new faces, the old ones are useless, worm-infested, and snake bitten. They created the problem, and are a major part of it; hence, they cannot be part of the solution. There must not be any recycling. In addition, the new faces must be racially blended;

those in waiting must become fully immersed in the nuances, rhythms, history, bonds, and wisdom of Indian, Black, and indigenous cultures, if there are going to be in a position to make a solid contribution to the harmony of the races in this country. The Indian and Black leaders do not need more exposure, and indoctrination, to their own —they already have that at the fingertips, and as a second skin. The challenge is to reach out, and then across to the other side —to learn, to understand, to identify with, and to clasp. And through these efforts, there must flow the care and compassion, which have been largely lacking in the political history of the past six decades.

The kind of new breed, and new leadership, needed is not in the PPP or PNC. Look closely —it is just not there! All that is there are men-and a few women-who conspire to share the spoils of power amongst themselves; and an unofficial version of personal power sharing between the two parties. Sure, there are thunderous bellows and the usual catfights when thieves fall out, but the PPP and PNC are one and the same. Can any sensible Guyanese differentiate between them where a dollar is concerned and self is involved? Some may say they are all that is around; well have them. The truth is that both are all that is wanted to be around. So what is left for this trapped, hapless society? Where do all roads lead?

CHAPTER XIII

THE ONLY WAY LEFT ....

"Sink or swim, live or die, survive or perish, I give my hand and my heart to this vote."
-Daniel Webster

At one time, and for the longest time, there was strong belief in the movement and progress of this society. That it had the capacity for a future as a nation, to realize the full richness of its potential. Not anymore.

Once, there was a deep faith in the paramountcy of patriotism, of putting the country and its people- all the people-first. It was that this would be the guiding force and the gravitational force field of leaders and other political contributors; that such a sustaining ideal and approach would help to overcome most obstacles, some frailties, and all the limitations inflicted by burdensome circumstances. Not anymore, for such faith has withered; and along with it the last forlorn tendrils of hope.

A Failure of Appeal, the Disappearance of Hope

For years, voice and pen joined with concerned others to exhort towards the bridge and hallway of discussion, the give-and-take of good

157

faith negotiation, the gaining and enabling of consensus, and the promise of destiny. Yes, at the end of all the believing and yearning and hoping, resided the faint echoes of the call of destiny –the vision of shared destiny. Not anymore, for that too is gone.

There has been no other thinking, no other vision but the "nationhood" now known and lived. And which was always lived before, no matter how fragile, or traumatic, or bleak. This thinking and vision has faded; there is no confidence that it can stand. Not anymore! Perhaps, not ever.

Previously there was support for the thread held out by the many dizzying forms of consensus government advocated. It was felt that whatever was agreed upon and finalized would lead to a better, more harmonious pathway forward for this hopelessly divided and deadlocked nation. A pathway that housed a ray of hope, a sense of belonging, and a chance for genuine lasting peace. That hope has fled too. It cannot be recaptured.

Now it is believed that any and all forms of governance previously touted-and supported-are doomed to failure. Whatever it is called-shared governance, power sharing, participatory democracy, grand coalition, people's partnership, federation, and so on-each has nowhere to go. None of them, no matter how configured, will last if it could get past the starting gate. None! For it will be susceptible to sabotage, manipulation, and circumvention; there will be the inevitable abandonment following, with little likelihood of reversion to the political conditions that existed before. It is abandonment which would lead to more discontent, more bitterness, and more unpleasantness. Why would this be so?

First, there is too much distrust at political leadership levels, at all levels; as this writing was being finalized, the Sunday newspapers identified a leading opposition parliamentarian complaining of being undermined by his own comrades. Second, this distrust is indicative of the acuity of the dishonesty and dishonor that prevails in political circles and beyond; of how diseased and degenerate the echelons of government, opposition, and parliament appear to be, and have de facto become. This distrust is utterly normal. Third, there is too much of "What is in it for ME? What am I going to get?" As always, the craven vulgar selfishness is so powerful, as to be irresistible; there is no space for the merest smidgen of patriotism, or public service. Fourth, no party wants to shed-and none more so than the numerically superior PPP-the cumbersome racial and emotional payload;

none has worked assiduously to dismantle-even ameliorate-the crippling psychological objections and resistance. Neither party has steeled itself, or has the mental audacity, to take a deep clean dive into the dirty racial maw. The will is lacking, the thinking sparse. For its part, the PNC has traveled part of the way down a long road in a struggle to find itself; it has a longer way to go. But it is where the PPP would never dare go. There is too much fear, too much to answer for, too much to lose.

So, the focus has been on vacillating and dissembling; on being cute and sacrificing residual goodwill and rarer good faith. Politicians think themselves cool and sophisticated, when in fact there are as sharp as wet blankets, just as easily recognizable, and about as useful. Thus, they give those who are still willing to listen **this farce about unity**; and the perpetuation of what has become a patented national fraud, a sick national joke. Amidst the splits and splinters, and where the only guarantees are standoff and failure, what is left? What is the answer? Where do all roads point and lead? Is there any other way?

The Bitter Pill of Partition (or racial nationalism)

It is an ugly word that makes the soul quail. It is a word that exhumes the disturbing history of India in 1947, and the birth of Pakistan. Yes, that one was ugly beyond the record of books and the extent of imagination. But it is what is left in Guyana for Guyanese to contemplate and implement. The only way forward for this nation is SEPARATION. The only solution believed left that makes sense, and offers a viable way out of the malaise and morass is PARTITION. It has been stated before, and even now this might be way before its time; but it is what is left as a reasonable, peaceable alternative. If not, then bloody revolution would raise its unwanted head sometime or the other, and then there would be no turning back. This is what the oracles of history, current circumstances and future promise reveal. All indications are that Indian Nationalism and Black Nationalism is the answer. It is this or the internecine warfare of conflict at some point in time. What exists cannot stand, will not stand.

The races need to go their own way, to their own places, to their own corner, with and among their own through some form of physical division and geographical reconfiguration; the how of that form is unknown at this time. They cannot live together in genuine, durable harmony, reciprocal respectful recognition, and deep-seated acceptance. Why? It is because the scheming Machiavellian politicians will not allow them to do so; because the resource pie is too small and too unfairly distributed; because the racial competition is too rank and ugly; and because the whole sordid history of this society never dissipates, but remains to impair powerfully the vision over every real-or imagined-instance of discrimination and loss. This history is never forgotten; it poisons and wounds the soul. And last because the mutual hostility and distrust are too ingrained and widespread. Certainly, both are muted and disguised, but they are present and they corrupt. What Guyanese have had is existence on a string; it is a transparent façade, the most obvious of frauds.

All of this has inhibited and dirtied and enfeebled. It is well to remember that Scriptural adage: A house divided against itself cannot stand. Guyana is a living example of its truth and accuracy for this place is irreversibly, incurably divided. There is the potential to sunder the nation apart in the most horrific of ways.

For once, the peoples of this nation must be honest with themselves and one another. Let the grim, inexorable realities be faced head-on. Let the poignant unassailable truths be recognized for what and how they are. What is present now, and what has been endured, retards at the individual and collective levels, and limits the realizing of potential -there is too much bickering, hostility, and malevolence. What is longed for is neither present nor real; only self-created mirages, followed by the accompanying endless disappointments. Again, why?

It is that the respective racial views of the world that is-and should be-Guyana are different; that racial priorities and objectives are different; and that the leadership to take each racial bloc towards its own aspirations must be different, too. Different in that it must be of their own "maatee" or their own kith, their own kin.

No local politician will acknowledge this; or ever admit to any of this. For purposes of self-promotion and self-perpetuation, they will insist on yoking dogs and cats together. That is, aggressive dogs and rebellious cats. To be sure, there will be periods of calm, but always there is the threat of eruption and harm. Always. And, it does flare into open conflict from time to time, which only intensifies the ill-will, and contributes further to the miasmic swamp of never-ending rancor. Clearly, this is counterintuitive and counterproductive. Said more bluntly, it is the height of stupidity, as well as wearying and destructive. Separation and Partition is the answer. It should be done voluntarily. BUT THIS IS NOT GOING TO HAPPEN! It will be resisted, until it is too late. Thus change will be forced upon this nation by force of arms and circumstances.

Speaking of force of arms and circumstances, all one has to do is focus on two precedents —one distant, the other closer; the first officially arranged, the second through involuntary flight. Both were sinister and devastating; the wounds refuse to heal to this day. First, there was India in 1947, and what became India and Pakistan; the flame of religion and the heat of history transformed the time into a pyre for many. Second and closer to today, there was the 1994 Rwanda genocide; on this occasion of unparalleled viciousness, the underlying determinants were ethnicity and history. Guyana is about racial struggle and historical memory; it might arguably be even somewhat about the religious and cultural too. But the bottom line is that the same specter hovers; the same antipathy inflames and unravels. And the same wrenching, bitter dislocation is promised. For those who say "can't happen here" some more thinking is urged. Take off the blinders; prepare to see the light, and to discern. Start through the simple acknowledgement of the intractability between local political-more accurately racial-leaders; and then recognize the growing incompatibility between the two major local races. Forget about the surface, the presenta-tion, and the political correctness. Look deeper and farther.

It is not accidental that migrating Guyanese end up in the equivalent of partitioned enclaves in the place where they have the largest overseas presence. In New York, Indians gravitate towards Queens, and they over-whelm huge tracts of Richmond Hill and Ozone Park. Similarly, Black Guyanese take up residence in Brooklyn, and populate such sections as Flatbush and East New York. In both instances, this could very well be due to sponsorship roots and family pull. Regardless, this has worked well in the large melting pot for the once tortured races of this land; they flour-ish. But they maintain old hometown political loyalties, sometimes with a fanatical zeal, and there follows this shabby situation where leading Indian politicians mainly focus time and attention on the Indo-Guyanese presence in Queens; and their Black counterparts concentrate on the Black Guyanese presence in Brooklyn. The ancient divisions, feuds, postures, racial ideologies, and racial dogmatisms have crossed the Atlantic and found renewed life among so-called 'concerned' Guyanese. Nobody lets go: not leaders, not supporters. Nobody has grown, no one can change; it is a telling indication of how warped and skewed citizens are, perhaps always were.

The cushion of space and dispersion afforded by the great metropolises, such as New York and Toronto, has made for little difference in political outlook. The struggle for assimilation and the coming of prosperity abroad have not dulled the racial edges. The comfort of tribe and clan has only intensified the disappointments and frustrations in one camp, and accelerated the joy and celebration in the other. If this can take place from so far, with so much sacrificed, so much gained, and so much learned, and the same crude racial mentalities dominate, then what about here? Yes, how much more corrosive are matters within the ramshackle, inequitable, injurious confines of the local environment so rife with individual and collective failures? What hope is there left? What hope can there be ....?

Altogether, the mere thought, and now the public tabling, of separation and partition-and all that this represents-pummels, then tears the heart. But there is nothing left: There is nothing to workout, to agree upon, to venture together. What once might have been acceptable options, but were not attempted before, are not believed in now. It is too late in the day. Hence, it all comes down to this: No justice, no peace! No equity, no solidarity! No brotherhood, no nationhood! Partition or revolution! All that is left are two scorpions in a bottle, and those final fateful words from Joseph Conrad's *Heart of Darkness* –"the Horror, the horror."

EPILOGUE

One Nation, One People, One Destiny

Really! Is this who and how we are? Is this what Guyana is in its heart and collective soul? Is any aspect of this accurate?

For some, racism is abhorrent to fundamental principles of morality and Christian ethos; rather sadly, these few are an isolated and overwhelmed minority. What is illuminating is that such debilitating behavior is rarely displayed in public. At both the private and official levels, it would be stridently denied and smoothly evaded, but it is rock-ribbed and visceral. Racism-deep and troubling-is not something disclosed even in the anonymity of polls and surveys. It is more a stealth strategy, but one with all the subtlety of a carving knife on the move. It is very present in Guyanese life.

What is present is an aggregation, a forced circumstantial fusion of many, perhaps, incompatible racial ingredients. Here is the uneasy sum of many parts, that never quite flow and blend into a solid, acceptable whole. There is no wholeness, no oneness, no unity of purpose or vision. There is little of that indefinable, binding sacredness that transcends crippling antagonisms, be they current, historical, or imagined. There is a paucity of compassion for struggling people from leaders, a lack of that special love for country from too many citizens, and an absence of thoughtful appreciation and respect for one another.

Instead, there is the tyranny of race, with its myriad remembrances that imprison in a grey, desultory existence. There are the countless memories that unsettle and agitate, as easily as the drift of a feather disturbed by the merest breath of wind. And to be sure, there are the immeasurable animosities that divide and park in camps of the abrasive and acrimonious. It is the abrasion and acrimony of mortal foes locked in close embrace, wrestling for supremacy, and dreading the damnation of losing. For losing in Guyana means a terminal deathlike racial existence. There has been no other experience lived. In spite of all the promises and projections, nothing else has been known.

Thus, "One People" is a mirage that magnetizes no one. It is stirringly rhapsodic to the senses, but not very likely to happen here, has not happened at all. What is it that has brought all the peoples together in a determined sustained drive towards a shared future? What was done, who was involved, where was it seen, and when did such occur? Let the cruel mindless games cease and the fancy words be spat upon, none of this has ever happened. None and never!

This business about "One Nation" has proven to be a political invention –a feeble and diseased one at that. It has not worked, does not work, will not work. It is because all political leaders and parties (all of them!) have dedicated their energies and interests to political ascendancy, which translates to the solidifying of racial monopoly. There is neither time nor place for real national unity; save for the vacuous and disingenuous. To political leaders, national unity has always been a far-off relation, and a poor one to boot.

The major races have their own favorite sports, support different local teams, adore separate heroes; all with a heavy racial cast. It is the same for national teams –national pride takes second berth to racial pride. There is grudging-if any-acknowledgment and recognition for the sterling contributions of men and women from the other side of the racial fence, whether cricket or rugby or boxing. They are there, they are known, but this is all there is to it. At best the appreciation is fleeting, casual or muted. Other than for the occasional, rare exceptions, this is the standard, the *modus vivendi*, in medicine, law, education, politics, arts, and a host of other fields of endeavor and disciplines. How can this place be rightly considered as "One Nation" when the races have limited appreciation for the sacred cultural mores of the next side? Or their concealed contempt for the religious pursuits and practices of the other? Or their irritation and distaste for music not their own? Again, how can this ever be seen as "One Nation?"

Last, there is nothing resembling a drive towards "One Destiny." Only the fevered pursuit of multiple ones (lots of them unlawful) conjured and nurtured in competing and conflicted breasts. Each race imagines and embarks on journeys apart, from different points, at separate times; and with destinations specific to its own visions. The pace is different, the load unique, the company homogenous. And it is all irreparably linked to the attainment of power, and the concomitant trajectory of race with all that this means for dominance, and access to the rich harvest of spoils.

Think of this: For the most part, Black teachers tutor and mentor the nation's children; Black policemen safeguard the nation's peoples; and Black nurses care for the sick and the elderly. They are good enough for all these things and more. But they are not good enough to sit at the table of inclusivity and decision making. When there should be grand ideas on how to build lasting bridges, on how to extend the hands of inclusivity, there is the absurdity and tawdriness of "ah yuh waan dem black man guh back in powah?" Here it is that somewhere between thirty to forty percent of a people has no say in charting its journey, in voicing its vision, and in sharing the content of its own desired destiny, and there is this fairytale about "One Destiny." How can this be when so many have been reduced to the ignominy of non-existence, and the jittery silence of converted lambs? Or is the reality closer to lurking panthers? Regardless, somebody-every thinking somebody-must ponder whether this matter of "One Destiny" is real; or one more mindless political vision, one more labored artificial construction, which has no chance of going anywhere, or achieving anything.

Clearly, this is society bedeviled by opposites instead of similarities; where the common ground that should bind is avoided and ignored; where the things that enrage and enfeeble are prioritized; where the comfort of a good neighbor has metamorphosed into the presence of a threat, and the existence of an enemy.

When all is said and done, argued and accepted and discarded, the stirring national vision encompassed in the words of "One People, One Nation, One Destiny" has neither been embraced nor pursued nor realized. Not before, not now. Maybe not ever. The record of local history speaks for itself: There has been neither substantial foundation planted, nor sturdy building blocks erected in the past or the present. What stares in the face and consciousness is the specter of a shaky perilous future. It is a small miracle that this country has somehow managed to hold together as one; it does so by a shoelace. It is a larger miracle that the racial volcano has not yet ruptured and exploded in the fullness of its fury and power. It struggles against its fragile restraints ...

I leave with the words of Robert F. Kennedy when he learned of the killing of Martin Luther King. He encouraged his audience to "say a prayer for our country, let us pray for the people." I say it is right to pray for ourselves, too. Now it is time to go.

www.ingramcontent.com/pod-product-compliance
Lightning Source LLC
Chambersburg PA
CBHW050121280326
41933CB00010B/1192